Policies and Practice

A Focus on Higher

Education Retention

American Association of State Colleges and Universities

.

Contents

Foreword

Gay M. Clyburn
Director of Communications
American Association of State
Colleges and Universities

While courts and some policymakers are challenging the tools used to attract and admit minorities and other underrepresented students to public university campuses, higher education administrators are also facing the challenge of ensuring that student learning and achievement support these students once they are admitted. These challenges are tied not only to emotional and social sentiments, but also to economic realities and misperceptions. Access, inclusion, and equity—and the methods used to ensure them—are evaluated in terms of cost and fiscal accountability at the expense of our nation's future.

While affirmative action and minority scholarships are debated, negated, and legislated in courts, board rooms, and state houses, funding for the support services to retain and graduate some of these same students is also at risk. It is within this tenuous environment that the American Association of State Colleges and Universities (AASCU) initiated a national retention project, two videoconferences, and a working group on access, inclusion, and equity to help its member campuses ensure that all citizens are included in the benefits available at public higher education institutions.

The association's projects addressing diversity issues were developed as part of one of six strategic planning goals. The AASCU/Sallie Mae National Retention Project, begun in 1992, was created in response to state expectations for more accountability (report cards and performance funding initiatives to monitor the return on scarce state resources) and federal reporting requirements on graduation and retention in Student Right-to-Know legislation. The first videoconference, "Constructing Effective Learning Environments: Retention Strategies for Campus Diversity," produced in 1995, was in response to information collected by AASCU campuses through the Retention Project. Although participation by minorities and other underrepresented groups had increased significantly, these same students were not staying in school and graduating with the same success as white students. (Unanswered questions from this event gave us the idea for this book.) African American and Hispanic students were about half as likely as their white peers to complete four years of college. The project also found that many institutions weren't tracking student achievement by gender, ethnicity, or transfer status. Not only did the project survey member institutions to determine successful retention programs, it also tracked student achievement by institution by gender, ethnicity, and transfer status.

The second videoconference, "Going Beyond Affirmative Action," produced in 1996, was to prepare campuses for the possibility that they would not have affirmative action as a tool to ensure access. By early 1996, some 17 states had legislation pending that would weaken or eliminate affirmative action. In July 1995, the University of California Board of Regents prohibited the use of "race, religion, sex, color, ethnicity, or national origin" as criteria in its employment and contracting practices and barred any reference to race or gender in admissions as of 1997. Proposition 209 put the state behind the regents.

That was also the year that *Hopwood* v. *Texas* barred the University of Texas law school from using racial preferences in admissions. Texas later ended minority scholarship programs, figuring the ruling applied to financial aid as well. The *Hopwood* ruling also banned admissions on the basis of race in Louisiana and Mississippi. Other lawsuits have followed.

In addition, lawmakers in several states are taking a hard look at funding for remedial education at the postsecondary level. California, where 60 percent of freshmen take remedial classes, will stop offering those classes by 2007. The State University of New York, where 29 percent of freshmen take remedial courses, may require that students take them at community colleges. Remedial education is one way to help at-risk students stay in college.

The mood of the country seemed then and seems now to be one of cost cutting at the expense of educational access. Many policymakers seem to be able to overlook the need to help any person who is denied or excluded opportunities—and thus benefits—because he is disadvantaged. Minorities, immigrants, and the poor are the groups from which come a disproportionate number of this nation's citizens who are faced with educational and economic uncertainty. AASCU determined that there was a need to develop statements to help the association and its members convince others to reverse the view that education is a private benefit rather than a benefit to society as a whole. In 1996, AASCU convened a working group on access, inclusion, and equity (it started out as a working group on diversity but changed its name to better reflect the work undertaken). Chaired by Dr. Alice Chandler, president emerita of the State University of New York, New Paltz, the 17-member group developed a policy statement for AASCU campuses, and Dr. Chandler wrote a policy paper, *Access, Inclusion and Equity: Imperatives for America's Campuses*. Both documents addressed retention of minority students and faculty as well as enrollment and recruitment. In the conclusion of the paper, Chandler notes:

> College and university presidents are on the firing line. They have the training and responsibility to look thoughtfully at the strengths and weaknesses of American society and to serve as pathfinders and guardians for that future. The current downsizing and downgrading of higher education requires of them the courage to argue for access and to argue that claim on behalf of a rapidly changing student body. They also have a responsibility to recruit that new student body, as well as the more traditional one, to nurture its abilities, to strive for a faculty representative of the true American talent pool, and to foster the values of diversity and inclusion on which the future of America must rest. College and university presidents can help to clarify and moderate the current rancor over equity by seeking equity as a normal condition on their own campuses and by promoting equity in the wider community.

AASCU's work on access, inclusion, and equity continues with the publication of this book. The chapters—written by university presidents, a system administrator, a retention scholar, and the director of a center serving an inner-city community—look at equity as it applies to "fostering the values of diversity and inclusion" as well as ensuring educational achievement and success. They are published as assistance to those who share the same mission and to those who understand that we must recognize and nurture the potential in every student.

Introduction

"Retention Strategies for Campus Diversity," an interactive videoconference produced by the American Association of State Colleges and Universities at Old Dominion University in cooperation with the Public Broadcasting Service's Adult Learning Satellite Service (PBS/ALSS), was held in February 1995 with some 328 sites participating. AASCU presidents—Joel Jones of Fort Lewis College (Colo.) and Vera King Farris of The Richard Stockton College of New Jersey—were part of the on-site panel, as was Vincent Tinto, associate director of the National Center for the Study of Teaching, Learning and Assessment at Syracuse University, and Noelia Vela, president of Evergreen Valley College (Calif.). Former Congresswoman Barbara Jordan (D-TX), Northeastern Illinois University sociologist Samuel Betances, and Manning Marable, head of the Columbia University Institute for Research in African American Studies, participated by video roll-in. The discussion was both thoughtful and lively, generating enough phone calls and faxes to block phone lines. This book, *Policies and Practice*, is an attempt to answer some of those questions and to further the discussion of successful retention practices on the campuses of public colleges and universities.

Two of the videoconference panelists—President Jones and President Farris—are chapter authors. Under their leadership, their institutions have become known for efforts in the area of retention. Other authors were chosen because of their association with the AASCU/Sallie Mae National Retention Project. Dr. Richard Richardson Jr. developed the model that AASCU used to delineate the status of retention efforts on its national survey of member campuses. All are leaders and have, on their campuses and through their good work, fostered student achievement and developed campus cultures to support diversity and learner-centered environments.

AASCU/Sallie Mae National Retention Project

Kenneth E. Redd
Research Associate
American Association of State
Colleges and Universities

Joyce A. Scott
Vice President for Academic
and International Programs
American Association of State
Colleges and Universities

Launched in 1991 through a grant from Sallie Mae, the American Association of State Colleges and Universities/Sallie Mae National Retention Project (NRP) was designed to engage college and university presidents and chancellors in leading their campuses to improve student retention and graduation rates, especially those of racial/ethnic minority students. Under the NRP, AASCU member colleges are surveyed each year and are asked to report their six-year graduation rates for full-time, full-year, degree-seeking students who entered as freshmen. The survey also asks the colleges to rate their campuses' views on administrative, academic, and assessment conditions that might affect these graduation rates.

This chapter describes the National Retention Project, the survey instrument, and other project activities. It also provides trends in the graduation rates of survey respondents from 1993 to 1996 and summarizes information on the administrative, academic advising, and assessment conditions that might influence graduation rates at these colleges.

The National Retention Project (NRP)

The NRP focuses on academic institutions as the object of inquiry rather than on student behavior. Richard C. Richardson's and Vincent Tinto's studies of the effect of campus culture on retention have guided project planning. The annual survey has been informed by Richardson's three stages of institutional evolution in addressing student retention. These stages are: *reactive*, focusing on recruitment, financial aid, admissions, and scheduling; *strategic*, focusing on outreach, transition, mentoring, enrollment, and residence hall activities; and *adaptive*, focusing on student assessment, offering learning assistance if needed, and adapting curricular content to embrace the variety of learning styles inherent in diverse student bodies. The adaptive stage is considered the most advanced, integrative stage.[1]

In 1993, 1995, and 1996, the surveys were expanded to draw upon Richardson's institutional self-assessment instrument. A series of questions were introduced through which researchers tried to delineate changes in campus culture by asking respondents to rate institutional conditions according to how well they described their own campus situation.

The survey questions were added because AASCU recognized that institutions must adapt to serve effectively an increasingly diverse and "nontraditional" student body. The project's fundamental premise is that student success is the responsibility of everyone on campus, from the president to faculty and staff, and that the burden of accommodation should not rest with the student alone.

Under the auspices of the project, AASCU has administered five annual graduation rate surveys to member institutions and has provided these institutions with feedback reports that compare their rates with their peer institutions', based on institutional enrollment size and geographic location. In addition to the surveys, AASCU members also have participated in activities designed to raise awareness of student persistence issues on campus and to assist presidents and their campuses in addressing related problems. Under the sponsorship of AASCU and Sallie Mae, there have been nine regional working conferences and five sessions at national meetings focused on student retention. In addition, the project has sponsored five publications, two national videoconferences on PBS, and two special projects designed to help campuses with relatively low six-year graduation rates improve their student outcomes. AASCU staff and representatives from the participating institutions also have made presentations at ten national meetings and have published chapters on project activities.

The AASCU/Sallie Mae National Retention Survey

The annual retention surveys became central to the project early. When AASCU administered the first survey in 1992, it found that only 78 of 188 responding institutions could provide the comprehensive cohort data required to complete the survey. This apparent lack of capacity raised concerns, not only about how well institutions could track students—and thus have an accurate picture of retention problems—but also about how well they could meet new accountability standards, such as those anticipated in the Student Right-to-Know Act reporting requirements to be implemented by the U.S. Department of Education in 1998. It was determined that an additional project purpose would be necessary: to help campuses improve their student tracking and reporting capabilities so they would be prepared to respond to emerging accountability requirements. To ensure relevance to this goal, AASCU opted to model the format under development by the National Center for Education Statistics (NCES) to report institutional graduation and persistence rates. At the same time, the association launched a project in collaboration with two other associations to consider and develop alternate reporting methodologies through a Joint Commission on Accountability Reporting (JCAR).[2]

AASCU has administered its survey to approximately 400 member institutions each year since 1992. The instrument comprises two parts: the first seeks information about state and campus academic and administrative conditions that might affect retention[3] and the second solicits data about student outcomes. The first survey (1992) solicited retention data—the number of students retained from first to second semester, from the freshman to the sophomore year, etc.—only to find so much variance between campuses' methods of tracking this information that comparisons were not possible. For this reason, AASCU researchers opted to use the six-year graduation rate as a proxy for retention in subsequent survey years[4] and to report analyses based on those responses. These rates are based on the number of first-time, full-time, full-year, degree-seeking freshmen who graduate within six years of entering college.

Since the NCES format was introduced, survey responses have increased steadily, rising from 188 (50 percent of member colleges) in 1993 to 290 (75 percent) in 1996. Similarly, the number of campuses that provided usable six-year cohort graduation rate data for first-time, full-time, degree-seeking students by sex and race/ethnicity increased from 63 percent of respondents in 1993 to 76 percent in 1996. Over the study period, the number of students represented in the respective full-time, first-time, degree-seeking freshmen cohorts increased from 121,903 in 1993 to 229,875 in 1996.

Analysis of the survey data reveals no appreciable change in overall six-year graduation rates during the study period; this is likely due to the expanding number of universities responding to the survey and to the short time period that the project covers. As Table 1 shows, the average graduation rate has increased slightly, from 40.6 percent in 1993 to 42.7 percent in 1996. Table 1 also reports the number of survey respondents, response rates, and average six-year graduation rates by sex and race/ethnicity from 1993 to 1996.

AASCU also examined graduation rates by campus admissions standards, types of institutions (historically black colleges and universities and minority-serving institutions[8] compared to all other institutional types), institutional enrollment size, and campus location. Admissions standards were drawn from the 1996 *Peterson's Guide to Four-Year Colleges*, which based institutional admissions selectivity on the high school class rankings and admission test scores of the majority of freshmen enrolled at each institution and on the percentage of applicants admitted to the colleges.

The admissions selectivity levels of participating AASCU members and the number of 1996 survey respondents within each level are as follows: *noncompetitive* (enrollment open to nearly all who apply, regardless of high school class rank or admission test scores), 20 respondents; *minimally difficult* (up to 95 percent of applicants accepted for admission), 30 respondents; *moderately difficult* (up to 85 percent of applicants accepted), 150 respondents; *very difficult* (approximately 60 percent of applicants accepted), 4 respondents. None of the NRP survey respondents were in the *most difficult* category (30 percent or less of applicants accepted). Admissions standards were missing for 12 of the respondents.

Admissions selectivity appears to have some influence on graduation rates, as the institutions with relatively high graduation rates also had more stringent

Table 1. Six-Year Graduation Rates for First-Time, Full-Year, Full-Time Freshmen in Degree-Seeking Programs

	1993 (Fall 1986 Freshmen Cohort)	1994 (Fall 1987 Freshmen Cohort)	1995 (Fall 1988 Freshmen Cohort)	1996 (Fall 1989 Freshmen Cohort)
Estimated Number of Surveyed Institutions	380	380	380	379
Number of Responding Institutions	188	200	258	283
Number of Responding Institutions with Usable Data	119	165	194	216
Survey Response Rate (1)[5]	49.5%	52.6%	67.8%	74.7%
Survey Response Rate (2)[6]	31.3%	43.4%	51.0%	57.0%
Overall	40.6%	40.8%	43.2%	42.7%
Male	36.7%	35.8%	38.6%	38.0%
Female	44.0%	43.6%	46.0%	45.3%
Nonresident Alien	38.3%	37.1%	34.6%	36.3%
Black, Non-Hispanic	29.1%	28.1%	31.7%	30.4%
American Indian/ Alaska Native	26.9%	24.6%	29.0%	28.3%
Asian/Pacific Islander	42.6%	41.4%	39.5%	40.6%
Hispanic	29.7%	29.5%	28.2%	29.3%
All Minority Students[7]	31.1%	30.1%	32.0%	31.9%
White, Non-Hispanic	43.4%	41.7%	45.6%	44.9%

admissions criteria. As Table 2 shows, the average graduation rate in 1996 for the very difficult institutions was 57.9 percent, compared to 44.8 percent for moderately difficult colleges, and just 33.3 percent for minimally difficult colleges. Graduation rates for minority students were also generally higher at more selective institutions.

Data comparing six-year graduation rates at special mission institutions (minority-serving institutions) and all other institutions within the AASCU sample appear in Figure 1 (p. 13). The number of minority-serving institutions participating in the survey remained about the same between 1993 and 1996, although the actual respondents did change. In both years, although the total six-year graduation rates at other institutions exceeded those at minority-serving institutions, outcomes for minority students were similar in both years and at both types of institutions.

However, minority graduation rates were higher at public historically black colleges and universities (HBCUs) than at all other institutional types (*see Figure 2, p. 14*). In addition, HBCUs showed a greater improvement in overall graduation rates over the four-year period. The rates for these institutions increased by 6.7 percentage points, compared to 2.1 percentage points at all other institutions.

Institutions with higher-than-average overall graduation rates often show higher-than-average rates for racial/ethnic minority students as well. On the 1996 survey, 70 institutions reported six-year graduation rates at or above 45 percent. The overall average graduation rate for these campuses was 55.6 percent, with an overall average of 57.3 percent for white students and 43.5 percent for racial/ ethnic minority students.

Among these 70 institutions, 24 campuses reported that ethnic/minority students made up at least 9 percent of their graduating classes. Twenty-one of these campuses showed higher graduation rates for white students than for racial/ ethnic minority students, while three campuses reported just the opposite. Comparison of six-year rates between white and racial/ethnic minority students on the 21 campuses showed differences ranging from a high of 34.4 percentage points to a low of 0.9 percentage points, with an overall average differential of 12.5 percentage points. At the other three campuses, the graduation rates of racial/ethnic minority students exceeded those of white students by 0.8 to 4.9 percentage points.

Table 2. Six-Year Graduation Rates for Full-Time, Full-Year, Degree-Seeking Freshmen, by Institutional Admissions Selectivity, 1996[9]

	Missing	Very Difficult	Moderately Difficult	Minimally Difficult	Non-Competitive
Number of Institutions	12	4	150	30	20
Overall	39.1%	57.9%	44.8%	33.3%	32.8%
Men	33.7%	60.2%	40.2%	27.9%	28.5%
Women	42.3%	56.9%	47.1%	36.8%	36.5%
Nonresident Alien	46.7%	44.4%	37.0%	35.7%	27.0%
Black, Non-Hispanic	31.1%	57.4%	31.7%	31.9%	17.0%
American Indian/ Alaska Native	7.7%	100.0%	30.3%	18.7%	21.0%
Asian/Pacific Islander	30.4%	68.3%	42.4%	26.9%	28.7%
Hispanic	29.6%	35.9%	29.5%	18.1%	24.3%
All Minority Students[10]	30.8%	38.3%	33.3%	29.6%	19.6%
White, Non-Hispanic	43.6%	75.3%	46.9%	34.4%	35.1%

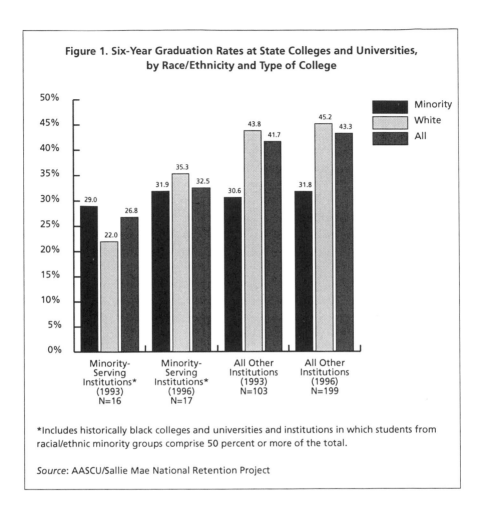

Figure 1. Six-Year Graduation Rates at State Colleges and Universities, by Race/Ethnicity and Type of College

*Includes historically black colleges and universities and institutions in which students from racial/ethnic minority groups comprise 50 percent or more of the total.

Source: AASCU/Sallie Mae National Retention Project

Graduation rates also differ by campus size and geographic location. Figure 3 (p. 15) shows that campuses in rural areas have higher rates than those in metropolitan and urban areas. Figure 4 (p. 16) suggests that a small or medium-sized campus may be beneficial to student retention.

Sixty-two campuses responded to the survey for four consecutive years. Table 3 (p. 16) shows that their aggregate six-year graduation rates did not change appreciably, although there was a slight (3.8 percentage point) increase in graduation rates for black students. Women continued to have higher six-year graduation rates than men, by 6 to 8 percentage points.

Among these 62 institutions, however, eight campuses showed steady improvement in their average graduation rates over the four years of surveys. The

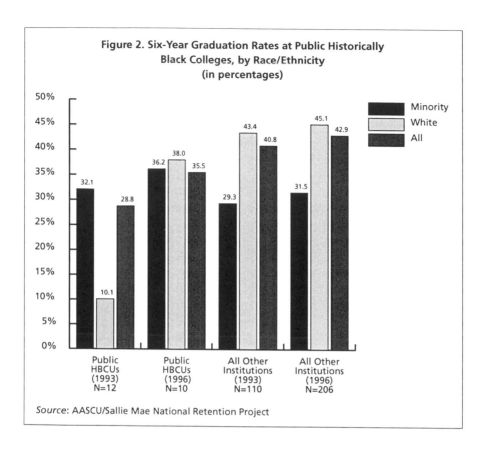

Figure 2. Six-Year Graduation Rates at Public Historically Black Colleges, by Race/Ethnicity (in percentages)

Source: AASCU/Sallie Mae National Retention Project

average overall graduation rate reported by these institutions increased from 42.5 percent in 1993 to 52.8 percent in 1996 *(see Table 4, p. 16)*.

In 1996, graduation rates for these institutions ranged from a high of 78.8 percent (up from 67.7 percent in 1993) to a low of 34.8 percent (up from 25.7 percent in 1993). Five of these institutions reported graduation rates greater than 50 percent. The average graduation rate for minority students at these institutions increased by more than 10 percentage points but still was much less than the rate for white students.

Thirty-two campuses responded every year and reported increases in their total graduation rates, even though they may have experienced a dip or anomaly along the way. As Table 5 (p. 17) shows, the average six-year graduation rate for these institutions increased slightly, from 39.5 percent in 1993 to 41.3 percent in 1996. Seven of these institutions had graduation rates of 50 percent or higher.

Once again, the average graduation rate for minority students at these colleges was much less than that for white students.

Not all of the campuses responding to the survey for four consecutive years showed increases in their six-year graduation rates. Twenty-three institutions reported fluctuations and drops in their graduation rates over the period, with the result that their reported rates in 1996 were lower than those in 1993. On average, fluctuations in institutional graduation rates ranged between 3 and 5 percentage points over the four years, but one institution showed a drop of almost 30 percentage points between 1995 and 1996. Four institutions showed steady declines year after year, from an aggregate six-year graduation rate of 34.9 percent in 1993 to an aggregate rate of 27.6 percent in 1996.

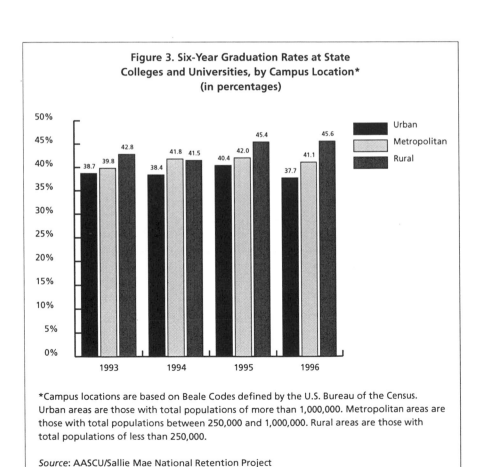

Figure 3. Six-Year Graduation Rates at State Colleges and Universities, by Campus Location* (in percentages)

*Campus locations are based on Beale Codes defined by the U.S. Bureau of the Census. Urban areas are those with total populations of more than 1,000,000. Metropolitan areas are those with total populations between 250,000 and 1,000,000. Rural areas are those with total populations of less than 250,000.

Source: AASCU/Sallie Mae National Retention Project

Table 3. Six-Year Graduation Rates for First-Time, Full-Time, Degree-Seeking Freshmen at Institutions That Responded to the NRP Survey for Four Consecutive Years[11]

	1993 (Fall 1986 Freshmen Cohort)	1994 (Fall 1987 Freshmen Cohort)	1995 (Fall 1988 Freshmen Cohort)	1996 Fall 1989 Freshmen Cohort)
Overall	40.2%	38.6%	40.9%	40.2%
Male	36.2%	34.1%	36.7%	35.6%
Female	43.7%	42.4%	44.3%	44.0%
Nonresident Alien	39.0%	36.0%	33.9%	40.9%
Black, Non-Hispanic	26.9%	27.7%	29.6%	30.7%
American Indian/Alaska Native	28.2%	23.5%	29.8%	21.1%
Asian/Pacific Islander	39.3%	39.5%	40.2%	40.3%
Hispanic	28.6%	27.7%	27.5%	27.0%
All Minority Students[12]	29.3%	29.2%	30.5%	30.6%
White, Non-Hispanic	42.5%	40.7%	43.5%	42.8%

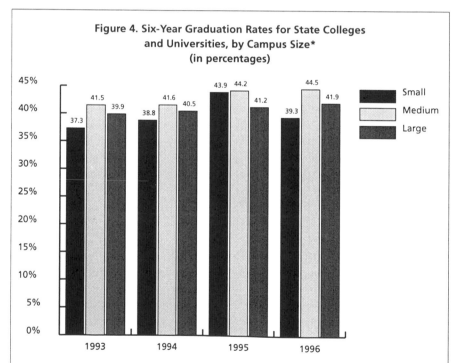

Figure 4. Six-Year Graduation Rates for State Colleges and Universities, by Campus Size*
(in percentages)

*Campus size is based on total headcount enrollment at each institution. "Small" colleges are those with enrollment of less than 5,000. "Medium" colleges have enrollments of between 5,000 and 11,999. "Large" colleges have enrollments of 12,000 or more.

Source: AASCU/Sallie Mae National Retention Project

Because all of these colleges and universities had chosen to participate in the project and had provided usable data on survey responses for the four years, one must assume that their administrators are monitoring student retention and graduation rates, a necessary condition to improving them. The question arises: What conditions on these campuses might account for the fluctuating or declining rates? Without an analysis of campus conditions and student demographics, a definite answer is not possible. Nevertheless, a review of these respondents shows that almost two-thirds are urban-serving institutions that customarily enroll large numbers of adult and nontraditional students. These students tend to take longer than "traditional" students to complete degree programs. In addition, approxi-

Table 4. Six-Year Graduation Rates for First-Time, Full-Time, Degree-Seeking Freshmen at Institutions That Responded to the NRP Survey for Four Consecutive Years and Increased Their Graduation Rates Every Year[13]

	1993	1994	1995	1996
Overall	42.5%	48.2%	50.4%	52.8%
Male	37.5%	42.4%	44.8%	47.6%
Female	46.5%	52.6%	54.7%	56.8%
Nonresident Alien	50.0%	53.8%	42.9%	42.6%
Black, Non-Hispanic	28.8%	34.0%	33.3%	36.1%
American Indian/Alaska Native	31.6%	35.7%	45.0%	39.5%
Asian/Pacific Islander	45.5%	46.0%	48.6%	53.4%
Hispanic	27.5%	35.8%	39.6%	40.8%
All Minority Students[14]	32.1%	37.0%	39.2%	42.4%
White, Non-Hispanic	44.2%	50.1%	45.6%	55.2%

Table 5. Six-Year Graduation Rates for First-Time, Full-Time, Degree-Seeking Freshmen at Institutions That Responded to the NRP Survey for Four Consecutive Years and Increased Their Overall Graduation Rates[15]

	1993	1994	1995	1996
Overall	39.5%	40.2%	41.2%	41.3%
Male	35.7%	33.2%	36.2%	35.7%
Female	42.9%	40.9%	43.8%	44.3%
Nonresident Alien	34.7%	33.0%	35.0%	44.1%
Black, Non-Hispanic	27.1%	28.7%	30.8%	32.6%
American Indian/Alaska Native	20.6%	23.2%	34.4%	26.1%
Asian/Pacific Islander	35.8%	38.7%	39.4%	38.0%
Hispanic	29.4%	28.9%	25.9%	26.8%
All Minority Students[16]	28.1%	29.4%	30.6%	31.7%
White, Non-Hispanic	41.4%	38.7%	42.1%	42.2%

mately one-third of the campuses have recently undergone substantial reorganization or changes in administration. Whether these are factors that contribute to changes in graduation rates requires more thorough investigation, but such conditions do affect campus climate and could reasonably be expected to have some influence on student persistence.

Administrative, Academic Advising, and Assessment Conditions

The NRP survey also asked institutions to describe several administrative, academic advising, and assessment conditions on their campuses that might have affected graduation rates. These conditions were based on the three stages of institutional development described earlier. Respondents indicated the extent to which these conditions described practices at their institutions. The responses were recorded on a Likert scale which ranked institutional self-assessments from 1 (not descriptive) to 5 (very descriptive).

To determine which of these conditions might have had a positive effect on graduation rates, the responding institutions were divided into two groups based on their 1996 rates. Selection into the groups was based on the average and standard deviation of the graduation rates of the 1996 survey respondents. Because the average rate was approximately 43 percent and the standard deviation was 13 percentage points, the high-rate colleges were those that had graduation rates of 56 percent or higher (43+13); the "low-rate" colleges were those with graduation rates of 30 percent or lower (43-13).

Twenty-nine institutions were identified as having graduation rates of 56 percent or higher, while 46 colleges had rates of 30 percent or lower. The average graduation rate for the high-rate colleges was 63.6 percent, compared to 24.5 percent for low-rate institutions. The average graduation rate for minority students at high-rate colleges was 49.5 percent, versus 21 percent at low-rate institutions. Among white students, the average graduation rate at high-rate colleges was 65.5 percent, versus 25.8 percent at low-rate institutions. More than 85 percent of the high-rate colleges had selection criteria rated at moderately difficult or higher (i.e., more selective), while 46 percent of the low-rate colleges had either noncompetitive (open) enrollment or minimally difficult enrollment criteria.

Table 6 (p. 20) shows a comparison of selected campus administrative, academic advising, and assessment conditions, based on the responses of high-rate and low-rate colleges. The percentages in the table are based on the numbers of institutions in each group that indicated the campus conditions were descriptive or very descriptive of their campuses.

As the table shows, nearly the same proportion of high-rate and low-rate institutions—86.2 percent versus 87 percent—said that *retaining and graduating more students is one of the top three priorities of campus administrators* was descriptive or very descriptive of their campuses. However, 62 percent of the high-rate institutions said that *the campus meets state goals for student graduation* was descriptive or very descriptive, compared to just 17.4 percent of the low-rate campuses.

Several academic advising conditions also may have been indicative of institutions with high graduation rates. More than 79 percent of the high-rate colleges said that providing orientation programs that address issues of cultural sensitivity was descriptive or very descriptive of their campuses, compared to about 54 percent of the low-rate institutions. Furthermore, 62 percent of the institutions with high rates said that providing an early alert system for students identified as being in academic difficulty was descriptive or very descriptive of their colleges, compared to just 41 percent of colleges with lower-than-average graduation rates. And nearly 83 percent of the high-rate colleges said that providing community college transfer students with accurate and timely course selection and financial aid information was descriptive or very descriptive of their institutions, compared to 69.5 percent of the colleges with lower graduation rates.

On the other hand, approximately 80 percent of the low-rate colleges said that *students identified as lacking the competencies required for entry-level courses receive appropriate instruction in basic skills, academic advising, and tutoring* was descriptive or very descriptive of their campuses, compared to 65.5 percent of the high-rate institutions. However, the institutions with the higher graduation rates also had higher admissions selection criteria. Thus, a lower proportion of the students enrolled at high-rate institutions likely required basic skills courses.

Campuse's efforts to assess student progress also appeared to play a role for institutions with higher graduation rates. Nearly 90 percent of the high-rate colleges said that *senior administrators regularly monitor information about progress in increasing retention and graduation rates of students* was descriptive or very descrip-

Table 6. Selected Responses to the Administrative, Academic Advising, and Assessment Conditions Section of the 1996 NRP Survey for High-Rate and Low-Rate Institutions

Campus Condition	Percentage of "High-Rate" Institutions That Said Condition Was Descriptive or Very Descriptive	Percentage of "Low-Rate" Institutions That Said Condition Was Descriptive or Very Descriptive
Retaining and graduating more students is one of the top three priorities of campus administrators.	86.2	87.0
The campus meets state goals for student graduation.	62.0	17.4
The campus provides community college transfer students with accurate and timely information about course planning, financial aid, and transfer requirements.	82.8	69.5
The campus orientation program for new students addresses issues of cultural sensitivity.	79.3	54.2
Students in danger of failing are identified by an early alert system and receive timely advising and assistance.	62.0	41.3
Students identified as lacking the competencies required for entry-level courses receive appropriate instruction in basic skills, academic advising, and tutoring.	65.5	80.4
The campus measures and reports on student outcomes from the course, program, and after-graduation accomplishments.	58.7	41.4
Senior administrators regularly monitor information about progress in increasing retention and graduation rates of students.	89.6	69.3

tive of their institutions, compared to 69.3 percent of the low-rate colleges. And nearly 59 percent of the high-rate institutions indicated that measuring student outcomes and post-graduation accomplishments was descriptive or very descriptive of their institutions, compared to just over 41 percent of the low-rate colleges.

These administrative, academic advising, and assessment conditions might be important in describing the reasons for the differences in graduation rates between high- and low-rate institutions. However, these results should be read with caution, since other factors and data that are not collected by the survey instrument (such as student financial aid) also may have affected graduation rates. It is also possible that institutional admissions selectivity criteria may have played a greater role in graduation rates than campus administrative and academic conditions.

Conclusion

With support from Sallie Mae, AASCU developed the National Retention Project to engage college and university presidents and chancellors in leading their campuses to improve student retention and graduation rates, especially the rates of racial/ethnic minority students. Among the tools used to promote these objectives were an annual survey, regional retention conferences, national videoconferences, special projects, and publications. Through the conferences, projects, and publications, AASCU disseminated strategies that institutions could use to improve their graduation rates and created networks of support among campuses committed to similar retention goals. These initiatives have had good results, engaging university presidents, deans, faculty, and students in a national conversation about how to promote and support student success and sensitizing campuses to the many factors that can contribute to better retention.

Survey results over the five project years are less encouraging, however, as they show—in the aggregate—only marginal improvement in six-year graduation rates, the proxy selected for student retention. These results also show that institutions with greater admissions selectivity were more likely to have higher graduation rates. These findings raise an important question for AASCU schools that have access-related missions or open admission policies: Is the connection between admissions selectivity and student persistence to graduation so strong that institutions with more liberal admissions policies cannot expect to make appreciable gains in student retention?

Of all the survey participants, only eight campuses showed steady improvement in graduation rates over the period. In the aggregate, their rates increased by 10.3 percentage points for both white and racial ethnic/minority students. In the context of overall outcomes, these results are exceptional. They bespeak unusual institutional effectiveness in managing student retention and merit further study.

Another 32 institutions showed overall improvement. However, their improvements were slight from year to year and gave a cumulative increase of less than 2 percentage points in the aggregate. Graduation rates for white students at these colleges increased by only 0.8 percentage points, while rates for racial/ethnic minority students increased 3.6 percentage points. This suggests that at least some of the strategies employed by these campuses to improve student retention are having a positive effect, particularly as they relate to minority students.

Based on survey results and campuses' reported experiences in addressing issues of student retention over the five years of the project, it becomes evident that improving students' retention and graduation rates is neither a short-term nor a simple proposition. Improving campus performance in this complex area depends on many factors: campus leadership, campus climate, administrative stability, administrative functions such as tracking and monitoring student progress, and the extent to which an institution—including faculty and staff—has been able to adapt to meeting the support needs (orientation, tutoring, advising, transfer assistance, etc.) of its particular student body. Any campus wishing to improve its performance in student retention must make a long-term commitment to the endeavor and be prepared to change the campus climate and services to be responsive to its students' needs. There is no quick fix, nor is there any universal fix in student retention. Each institution must address its own special constituency and its special needs effectively.

Notwithstanding the slight improvements documented for AASCU members' six-year graduation rates, the National Retention Project has had positive outcomes. It has focused members' attention on issues of student retention and their complexity. It has made campuses aware of the types and details of student information that will be required under the Student Right-to-Know reporting conventions, with the result that the number of campuses able to provide this information has almost doubled in four years.

Finally, it has brought to the fore important research questions about the relationship between campus conditions and student outcomes, questions that can improve our knowledge about student retention. What strategies have been most effective in promoting student retention to graduation? What conditions have accounted for retaining racial/ethnic minority students successfully on those few predominantly white campuses that did better than others in graduating these students? What conditions prompt declines in student retention? How do changes in institutional governance, organization, or administration affect student persistence and degree attainment? And finally, given the observed relationship between admissions selectivity and student persistence to graduation, how do institutions with more liberal admissions policies make appreciable gains in student retention?

Notes

[1] R. C. Richardson Jr., "A Model of Institutional Adaptation to Student Diversity," in *Achieving Quality and Diversity*. New York: ACE/Macmillan, 1991.

[2] Created in 1994 by the American Association of State Colleges and Universities (AASCU), the American Association of Community Colleges (AACC), and the National Association of State Universities and Land-Grant Colleges (NASULGC), the Joint Commission on Accountability Reporting (JCAR) was established to develop common ways of presenting easy-to-understand comparable information. The reporting conventions developed by JCAR provide a uniform means to report: (1) for all institutions and programs: student advancement toward completing educational goals; student charges (costs); graduation rates; and transfer rates; and (2) for vocational, occupational, and professional programs: licensure pass rates; placement rates; and full-time employment rates. The above reporting convention recommendations were released in November 1995.

[3] This portion of the survey draws from R. C. Richardson Jr., D. A. Matthews, and J. E. Finney, *Improving State and Campus Environments for Quality and Diversity: A Self-Assessment*. Denver: Education Commission of the States, 1992.

[4] President Harley Flack of Wright State University (OH) suggests that this choice disadvantages campuses that serve large numbers of part-time or adult students who

may enroll intermittently or who do not intend to complete a bachelor's degree. President Flack calls for a change in the paradigm of retention in favor of an approach that uses multiple, nontraditional measures such as assessment of learning outcomes and benchmarking according to institutional mission.

[5]Based on the total number of responding institutions.

[6]Based on the number of institutions with usable graduation rate data for first-time, full-time, degree-seeking freshmen.

[7]Does not include nonresident alien students.

[8]By definition of the U.S. Department of Education, minority-serving institutions (in addition to those with historical designation such as historically black colleges and universities) are those whose student bodies comprise at least 50 percent students from racial/ethnic minority groups.

[9]Admissions selectivity standards are based on the 1996 *Peterson's Guide to Four-Year Colleges*.

[10]Does not include nonresident alien students.

[11]Based on 62 survey respondents who provided usable graduation rate data for four consecutive years of the NRP.

[12]Does not include nonresident alien students.

[13]Based on eight survey respondents.

[14]Does not include nonresident alien students.

[15]Based on 32 survey respondents.

[16]Does not include nonresident alien students.

Bibliography

A Need Answered. Washington, DC: American Association of State Colleges and Universities, 1995.

JCAR Technical Conventions Manual. Washington, DC: American Association of State Colleges and Universities, 1995.

Richardson, R. C. Jr., "A Model of Institutional Adaptation to Student Diversity," in *Achieving Quality and Diversity*, New York: ACE/Macmillan, 1991.

Richardson, R. C. Jr., D. A. Matthews, and J. E. Finney. *Improving State and Campus Environments for Quality and Diversity: A Self-Assessment*. Denver: Education Commission of the States, 1992.

Toward More Systemic Retention Strategies

Richard C. Richardson Jr.
Professor
Division of Education Leadership
and Policy Studies
Arizona State University

Mary Aleta White
Doctoral Student
Arizona State University

If retention means keeping students around long enough so that some reasonable proportion of them earns a degree, what is long enough and what is reasonable? Surely those who made the decision to change our system of higher education from meritocratic to mass access during the late 1960s and early 1970s understood high attrition rates as part of the price of giving everyone the chance to attempt higher education. Until the quality-conscious 1980s, community colleges justified high attrition rates by emphasizing the student's "right to fail." We do not expect the same survival rates for those who undergo high-risk open-heart surgery as for those admitted for a tonsillectomy. Why shouldn't we expect lower survival rates among today's higher-risk students?

According to U.S. Department of Education estimates, 45 of every 100 students entering four-year schools eventually will earn a degree; the proportions have not changed over the last 100 years.[1] Apparently, our system gets about the same results regardless of the qualifications of those who enter. Sooner or later, someone was bound to challenge a process that produced such consistent results regardless of student input or costs. In the accountability-oriented 1990s, a growing number of states have begun examining outcomes and reporting institutional results to legislators and the general public. This practice raises concerns among institutional leaders in part because of the absence of generally accepted standards for performance.

While total outcomes may be little changed, different types of institutions report very different retention and graduation rates. Ivy League institutions have four-year graduation rates in the mid 1990s. The U.S. academies at West Point and Annapolis graduate between 70 and 80 percent of those they admit in four years. The University of California, Los Angeles has a five-year retention/ graduation rate for regularly admitted Asian Americans and whites in the high 60s; comparable figures for African Americans and Latinos are in the high 40s or low 50s. Four-year City University of New York institutions graduate about 30 to 35 percent of their first-time entering freshmen in five years and retain another 20 percent. The University of Texas at El Paso (UTEP) reported five-year retention/ graduation rates for the class entering in 1980 of about 32 percent. Significantly, Hispanics outperformed whites by a slight margin.[2]

Which among these institutions are doing well? Which are doing poorly? How do we know? When we calculate retention statistics and use them to hold institutions accountable, what allowances should we make for such student characteristics as socioeconomic status, high school preparation, SAT or ACT scores, family responsibilities, having a first language other than English, living conditions, and employment?

Serving higher-risk students, as AASCU institutions historically have done, raises attrition rates, but systematic efforts to help them succeed can bring those rates back down. In 1988, UTEP found that it was achieving higher retention rates with "at-risk" students than with its regular student population. In a speech, UTEP's president rhetorically asked the faculty whether it wasn't time the university applied to the rest of its students the lessons learned in working with its "at-risk" population. Shortly thereafter, a UTEP faculty member argued in *The Chronicle of Higher Education* that UTEP's success with Hispanics had only been achieved by lowering standards.

The story illustrates how closely access, quality, and retention are bound together. It is virtually impossible to talk about one without considering the others. Concerns with retention spring not so much from unwillingness to accept the element of risk associated with trying to provide opportunities for everyone as from observations that current outcomes seem to enhance rather than eliminate advantages attributable to being born to Asian American or white parents. States can ill afford systems of higher education that widen existing disparities in social stratification along racial and ethnic lines.

The key retention issue is how to eliminate race- and ethnicity-related differences in retention and graduation rates while concurrently working to improve overall retention rates without sacrificing quality. The AASCU/Sallie Mae National Retention Project (NRP) reflects one major effort to come to grips with this challenge.

Insights From the National Retention Project

The surveys on student retention rates collected by NRP from member colleges and universities offer an interesting window on institutional performance. The data show practically no changes (.02 percent) in six-year graduation rates for the 64 campuses that responded all four years. However, the number of campuses with good, usable data has increased every year, as has the total number of campuses responding (300 in 1996). Graduation rates for African Americans and Native Americans increased about 3 percent during the same period, from 27.5 to 30 percent and from 25.1 to 28 percent, respectively. For Hispanics, graduation rates declined from 29.9 to 28.4 percent.

If we break respondents into groups, the picture changes. Eight campuses that provided information all four years increased graduation rates steadily, for a total of 10 percent for the period of the project. Another 46, while experiencing some sort of interruption along the way, nonetheless increased graduation rates on average for the four-year period by somewhat more than 2.5 percent. So 54 campuses are clearly improving, and some faster than others. Reported six-year graduation rates in 1996 ranged from 83 percent to 0 percent. There are still 53 institutions with graduation rates at or below 30 percent.

What kind of sense can we make from this data? First, 62 percent of those surveyed could provide six-year graduation rates; 59 percent provided the rates by gender and 58 percent by race. Clearly, most AASCU institutions now have the data systems and the sense of priority that allowed them to provide the type of comparative data the project required. But more than a third still lack the capacity to assess current performance in retaining students. We know that what gets measured improves. And so those campuses with the longest history of keeping track of retention are also among the most likely to report improved results.

Let's try to tease out some additional insights. Imagine for a moment a continuum of retention practices that is anchored at one end by incremental actions aimed at removing the barriers to participation for underrepresented groups through changes to admission practices, financial aid, or relationships with feeder schools. The far end of the continuum involves systemic transformational change aimed at: constructing improved learning environments through more effective teaching and learning practices; increasing faculty commitment to the success of all students; and providing learning assistance that bridges the gap between preparation, learning styles, and graduation. Somewhere between these two extremes lies a midpoint of institutional reform which aims at adaptive improvements to existing campus teaching and learning practices as well as an improving campus climate. Incremental strategies remove barriers to participation; adaptive strategies focus primarily on changing students; and transformational strategies are about changing institutions.

The goal of the National Retention Project was to encourage participating institutions to become more systemic in their retention strategies—that is, to move along the continuum away from incremental changes and toward institutional transformation. Was this goal realistic? What do the data suggest about how well it was attained?

In 1996, most AASCU institutions clearly were closer to the incremental than to the transformational end of the continuum. According to survey data, institutional efforts to fix the retention problem focused on recruiting better prepared students, supporting students with skill or content weaknesses, making higher retention and graduation rates a top administrative priority, maintaining ties to the K–12 community to support improved preparation of students, and monitoring progress in increasing retention and graduation rates. Former AASCU Retention Project Director Pamela Arrington reported that most retention strategies remain outside the institutional mainstream.

The problem with strategies focused on removing barriers to participation or on changing students is that they do not alter retention and graduation outcomes—or at least they do not alter them very much. According to Deming, 85 percent of the variance in outcomes is attributable to the way a system is designed and managed.[3] That leaves very little variance for individual change strategies to affect. If most of the institutions in AASCU's database have retention strategies that are not well integrated into mainstream academic operations, we should expect outcomes to remain essentially the same—perhaps a little better or a little worse, but essentially the same. This is what the data analysis revealed.

At the same time, growing numbers of AASCU institutions have moved or are moving toward becoming more strategic and adaptive, as evidenced by improved retention and graduation rates at 54 institutions. Our data almost certainly understate the number that have become more systemic in their retention efforts given lag times between actions and changing outcomes. Most retention initiatives focus on the critical high school-to-college transition and on the freshman year. Accordingly, we should expect a minimum five-year delay between the time a retention project begins and when graduation outcomes begin to improve. We have only four years of data for NRP.

The results for the 1996 survey illustrate two types of errors we should avoid in attributing meaning to NRP outcomes. We don't want to claim successes that would have happened anyway. But equally important, we don't want to reach erroneous conclusions about failure from outcomes the project could not reasonably have been expected to influence. Were more successful institutions already engaged in systemic efforts to improve retention at the time the project began? Did the project encourage and empower their efforts by recognizing and assisting them, thus increasing internal credibility? Were there other factors, such as more selective admission practices, that contributed to improved retention? Do some AASCU institutions believe they are already doing as well on retention as they need to? Does averaging data for institutions that aren't interested in improving retention rates with those that are distort the results for both? How would a small sample of institutions that improved compare to a similar sample of those that did not?

Such questions are not easy to answer, but trying to answer them is an important element in becoming more systemic. At the incremental end of the continuum, institutions offer retention programs whenever resources permit but often don't stay interested long enough to find out whether outcomes were affected. Not all institutions need the same types of strategies. Historically black colleges and universities (HBCUs) have few barriers to participation and supportive environments, but they may need to reform learning environments to provide greater assistance to the students they now attract, as distinct from those they attracted before historically white institutions became serious about recruiting from the same population. Institutions with retention rates of 60 percent or above and comparable graduation rates for all races and ethnic groups may need only incremental change, if that. Institutions that need only modest improvement can use strategic planning to shape gradual adaptive changes. Institutions with retention and graduation rates significantly below the norm for their type of setting or unacceptably large retention discrepancies related to race or ethnicity should think seriously about systemic change if they are interested in improving their game.

Becoming More Systemic

Most colleges and universities are segmented along functional lines.[4] Arizona State University has people responsible for getting students into college, others who try to be sure they get into the right classes, still others who focus on housing, health, and social life, people who organize and teach classes and report grades, staff who keep records and certify progress, and those who try to help students connect with a desired job. None of these functional areas can be held individually responsible for retention and graduation rates. Sometimes institutional leaders talk as if the faculty collectively should be held accountable, but no one has yet figured out how that can be managed.

Our plan for making all of this fit together involves organizing everyone into large functional groupings of related specialists who are presided over by vice presidents who, in consultation with the campus president, provide the necessary direction and coordination. Significantly, no one has the title of vice president for student retention. Hammer and Champy describe this organizational arrangement as "functional silos or stovepipes, built on narrow pieces of a process" in which people look inward toward their departments and upward to their leaders, but no one looks outward to the student.[5]

To cope with the dilemma that arises because colleges are being held accountable for a process for which no one is responsible, we establish cross-functional "retention committees" comprising representatives from each of the stovepipes even while we chuckle about the definition of a camel as a horse designed by a committee.

From this perspective, we can see that the AASCU Retention Project focused on improving the quality of services within each stovepipe while concurrently searching out ways to achieve synergy among them and to guide students to the right stovepipes at the right times. An interesting question might be whether it is possible to eliminate functional stovepipes entirely in favor of groups that actually have responsibility for students. This is the key question asked by transforming institutions.

Imagine for a moment that an interdisciplinary team of university professionals and support staff has responsibility for retaining a group of undergraduate students through the first two years of college and at the end of that time producing candidates who have made an appropriate career decision and who are fully prepared to enter their major of choice. Assume further that the team has to accomplish its task within existing cost parameters and that its first job is to design the program. The team will be rewarded and retained based on its success at improving retention and user satisfaction. If the team is able to reduce costs while improving outcomes, it will receive a bonus which its members will decide among themselves how to distribute. The team is collectively responsible for designing the process and is collectively accountable for the results. It is insulated from existing structures, reward systems, and disciplinary affiliations by a dean who understands her role as coaching and support rather than supervision or management.

Portland State University is one place where transforming strategies are at work. There, each of 20 members of a freshman inquiry faculty team drawn from departments across the university will devote two-thirds of their teaching to a general education program specifically designed around the needs of students. The program, taken by all incoming freshmen, incorporates team teaching, interdisciplinary programs and course clusters, integration of academic skills within course content, inclusion of diversity and multicultural themes across the curriculum, student community service, and enhancement of student-student and student-faculty interaction. Significantly, the new general education program will not be more costly than the way the institution previously has taught comparable courses.[6]

The new California State University campus at Monterey Bay has been planned around similar strategies, very different from the learning approaches traditionally used in other parts of the large, historically incremental enterprise of which it is a part.

Yet another example can be found in the efforts of colleges and universities to create undergraduate learning communities organized around cultural, vocational, or intellectual interests. Such communities cut across stovepipes by organizing the admissions process, social and residential experiences, and the learning experience around some common theme, such as high academic achievement, as in honors colleges, or cultural identity, as in the case of Native American or African American theme living and learning groups.

Within the adapting institution, strategic planning is used to align the pieces of a larger educational process fragmented by the way institutions are organized. The transforming institution focuses on redesigning programs and services to eliminate fragmentation. Beyond looking at the way institutions organize programs and services, we also can get some sense of where they are along the continuum by the questions they find important. Incrementally focused institutions worry about improving retention rates for high-risk students. Adapting institutions focus on improving retention and graduation rates for everyone. And transforming institutions address retention issues by improving the quality of undergraduate education.

Conclusion

The basic model for educating undergraduates followed by most institutions was designed around a much smaller and less diverse segment of the population than is currently found at most AASCU institutions. The model still works well for institutions that are highly selective, like UCLA and Stanford, or small and single purpose, like the California Maritime Academy. Most AASCU institutions, however, do not deal with highly selective student populations or narrow missions.

Can public colleges and universities engage in transformation in the absence of the type of threat to survival that motivated change among American businesses? Is undergraduate education at any AASCU institution sufficiently problematic to require transformation, or should most AASCU institutions pursue more modest improvements through strategic planning within an adaptive framework? Which questions are your institutions currently asking about student achievement? Which should you be asking?

Notes

[1]Tinto, V. *Leaving College: Rethinking the Causes and Cures of Student Attrition*. Chicago: The University of Chicago Press, 1987, p. 22.

[2]Richardson, R. C. Jr. and E. F. Skinner, *Achieving Quality and Diversity: Universities in a Multicultural Society*. New York: ACE/Macmillan, 1991.

[3]Deming, W. E. *Quality, Productivity, and Competitive Position*. Cambridge, MA: Massachusetts Institute of Technology, Center for Advanced Engineering Study, 1982.

[4]Kanter, R. M. *The Change Masters*. New York: Simon and Schuster, 1983. The author discusses the difference between segmented and integrated organizations and the consequences of each.

[5]Hammer, M. & J. Champy. *Reengineering the Corporation*. HarperCollins Publishers, 1993, p.28.

[6]White, C. R. *Portland State University Studies Program Executive Summary and Report*, Institutional Document, April 1994.

Looking at Maryland Higher Education: Teaching and Learning Practices and Student Retention

Pamela G. Arrington
Senior Staff Specialist
Division of Planning and Academic Affairs
Maryland Higher Education Commission

The purpose of this chapter is twofold: to acknowledge that substantial research exists on the social and academic variables that influence whether students stay in school or leave and to focus on the role of faculty in the success and the ongoing assessment and evaluation of student retention practices and programs.

Trends and Issues in Student Retention

Let's first look at support for retention efforts from outside the academy. Beginning in the 1980s, there was a movement in higher education toward effectiveness and accountability. The country's economic climate and how it played out at the state level was certainly a catalyst for this movement. Public concerns prompted calls from legislators to state coordinating boards for higher education and college administrators asking for more accountability on new program costs, financial aid programs, and other student support programs. An institution's retention and graduation rates became a measurable outcome of institutional accountability. Similarly, K–12 schools came under scrutiny in the 1970s and still are criticized for not teaching basic skills and for leaving graduates unprepared for postsecondary education. Indeed, many in higher education argue that retention and graduation rates would be greatly improved if students were adequately prepared for first-year college-level work. There is reason for concern. A recent study by the Maryland Higher Education Commission found that nearly half (47 percent) of all new students at Maryland public campuses who enrolled directly from high school needed some form of remediation, and 23 percent required assistance in two or more subjects.[1] Almost 60 percent of the first-time students at community colleges and one-fourth of those at public, four-year institutions received remediation.

In 1993, the federal government got involved in measuring higher education outcomes. The U.S. Department of Education required that states create State Postsecondary Review Entities (SPREs) to address institutional accountability and to include measures of student achievement. Fortunately, some would argue, Congress didn't fund the SPREs. However, getting ready for SPREs turned up the heat. Demands from state legislators for more accountability from postsecondary education continue as a result. This pressure is fueled, in part, by competition among higher education and other state funding priorities, like Medicaid and corrections, when state resources are either stagnant or dwindling.

Minority participation and success, however, dropped off the radar screens of many legislators as they looked at higher education outcomes. The State Higher Education Executive Officers (SHEEO) studied trends in state coordination and governance in a 1996 survey.[2] Interestingly, it found that there has been a significant decline since 1989 in the prioritization of minority student access and achievement (-.81). Respondents reported that state financial support, effectiveness and accountability, and instructional technology were the most important issues in 1996. In addition, efforts to recruit and retain students for diverse campus communities using special admissions criteria that included race as a criterion were challenged through the courts in Maryland, Texas, Louisiana, Mississippi, Alabama, and California.

Another trend emerged during this decade. In 1993, there was an increase in the number of African American (74.8 percent) and Hispanic (60.7 percent) students completing a high school education.[3] The number of Caucasian high school graduates stayed the same. The Hudson Institute projected that 85 percent of new entrants to the workforce in the 21st century will be minorities and women.

This information raised questions that required answers from higher education. Will these new workers have the necessary skills for jobs that are based on knowledge and that compete in a global economy? How well are colleges and universities preparing the new entrants to the workforce and retraining current workers? After surveying more than 2,500 Maryland employers, the Maryland Higher Education Commission found that by the year 2005, six in every ten job openings will require some form of education or training beyond high school.[4] Without minority recruiting and retention efforts, the needed populations would not participate in higher education at the rate required to support the workforce.

Statistics indicate that there is work to be done. Even though there has been an increase in tuition over the past decade, more high school graduates (from 49 percent in 1987 to 62 percent in 1993) are choosing to go immediately to college after high school graduation.[5] However, high school graduates from low-income families (50 percent) were less likely than graduates from high-income families (79 percent) to enroll in college.[6] Many of these freshmen will not graduate. In 1990, only one-quarter of first-year community college students were enrolled in some form of higher education the next year; about one-fifth of second-year community college students transferred to four-year colleges or universities.[7] In fact, it is very common for college students to enroll, leave, possibly return, or not finish within the expected time.[8]

Generally, low tuition levels at American Association of State Colleges and Universities (AASCU) schools and increased federal financial aid have supported higher levels of participation.[9] However, even with current levels of aid, many Americans are struggling to pay for college. Among dependent, full-time undergraduates attending public, four-year institutions, the average grant aid received was 29 percent of the average tuition and fees charged during the 1992–93 academic year. This ratio ranged from 80 percent for students from low-income families to 10 percent for those from high-income families.[10] The percentage of full-time students who work more than 20 hours a week has increased since the 1980s. This fact may affect whether students go on to complete college and/or lengthen the time they take to complete a degree. Half (52 percent) of bachelor's degree seekers who first enrolled on a full-time basis reported having completed the degree in five years, compared to less than 15 percent of those who first enrolled less than full time.[11] Other differences in access, participation, and progress noted in *The Condition of Education 1996* include the fact that traditional-age students (18 or younger) who enter postsecondary education are more likely than nontraditional-age students (age 20 to 29) to complete a bachelor's degree within five years (51 versus 19 percent) and are five times more likely to do so than students who enter at age 30 or later. Furthermore, students who begin in four-year institutions are much more likely to report completing a bachelor's degree in five years than those who begin in two-year institutions (57 versus 8 percent).[12]

According to NCES, from 1971 to 1995, the percentage of students completing high school increased 9 percentage points (from 77.7 percent to 86.9 percent); the percentage of high school graduates had completing at least some college rose nearly 19 percentage points (from 43.6 percent to 62.2 percent); and the percentage of high school graduates completing four or more years of college rose more than 6 percentage points (from 22.0 percent to 28.4 percent). Yet there are differences in the degree of educational attainment by race. While fewer black 25- to 29-year-olds (86.8 percent) had completed high school than their white counterparts (92.5 percent) in 1995, the gap between the percentage of blacks and whites completing high school narrowed between 1971 and 1995 from 23 to 6 percentage points.[13] Fifty-two percent of black high school graduates had completed some college in 1995, versus 65 percent of white high school graduates. Eighteen percent of black high school graduates versus 31 percent of white high school graduates had completed a bachelor's degree or higher. Considering the same cohort, NCES found that for 25- to 29-year-old Hispanics in 1995, 57.2 percent completed high school, compared to 92.5 percent of their white counterparts. Fifty percent of Hispanic high school graduates had completed at least some college, and 16 percent had completed a bachelor's degree or higher.

Because colleges and universities devote efforts to programs designed to recruit diverse students and to provide academic support services to diversely prepared students, the student body at colleges and universities has become increasingly diverse since the mid 1970s.[14] Minority students increased from 15 percent of all students in 1976 to nearly 22 percent in 1992. For example, African American students accounted for nearly 10 percent of the total enrollment at colleges and universities in 1992. Hispanics made up 7 percent, Asians 5 percent, and American Indians 1 percent of enrolled students. At most AASCU institutions, the student bodies comprise more students who attend part time, commute, are academically underprepared, and combine school with family obligations and financial difficulties. Thirty-six percent of all undergraduates (2,536,973) and 36 percent of all minority undergraduates (529,802) enroll at AASCU institutions. Retaining and graduating these students is challenging.

Across all institutional types, concern about student success is warranted. For the past three years, results from the AASCU/Sallie Mae National Retention Project found that six-year graduation rates hover around 40 percent; they were 40.6 percent in 1993 and 1994 and 43.2 percent in 1995. The six-year graduation rates for white students in 1993, 1994, and 1995 were 43.8, 42.6, and 46.1 percent, respectively. Graduation rates for minority students were significantly less. For black students in 1993, 1994, and 1995, the six-year graduation rates were 27.5, 29.8, and 31.7 percent, respectively. For Hispanic students, the six-year graduation rates for those years were 29.9, 30.5, and 29.4, respectively.

Campus Climate

Colleges and universities have paid a good deal of attention to those social and campus climate variables that make up the "institutional fit" paradigm.[15] Beginning in the mid 1970s, the dominant theme in retention research was that retention and attrition result from the interactions between students and the institution.[16] An institution's social environment plus the student's academic performance must be considered equally before an adequate, integrated understanding of the retention process is possible. Senior administrators and faculty must ask themselves, "Which of the institutional practices we employ are best for the students we have, and which institutional practices should we modify to better academically and socially involve our students?" For years, historically black colleges and universities (HBCUs) have promoted the fact that the African American students enrolled at these schools perceive a certain socially relevant comfort zone that accounts for their sustained student achievement. For example, African American undergraduates who attended HBCUs were more likely to aspire to an advanced degree than were students at other four-year colleges or universities.[17] Even at HBCUs, once the more selective campuses are removed from the data, retention and graduation rates are mediocre at best. Perhaps this supports the premise that social campus climate variables alone will not sustain high retention and graduation rates over the long haul. Campuses must focus on both social and academic variables, especially teaching and learning practices that involve faculty in campuses student retention efforts.[18]

The literature indicates numerous programs for varied student populations that address access, academic, and social support services to include mentoring programs, pre-college summer bridge programs, orientation programs, learning communities, use of learning technologies, tracking systems, and two-year to four-year college student transfer articulation programs. Significant documentation supports these themes. Most recently because of special federal funding opportunities with organizations like the National Aeronautics and Space Administration, the National Science Foundation, and the Department of Health and Human Services, many campuses have implemented programs to recruit and retain traditionally underrepresented student groups to major in disciplines such as science, engineering, mathematics, and health sciences. However, the evidence of colleges and universities adapting their teaching and learning practices in some comprehensive, structured, campus-wide approach to address diversity issues and to address the needs of diversely prepared students is less frequent.

Teaching and Learning Practices

The frequency and quality of student-faculty interactions has a significant effect on student success. Using Tinto's model of academic and social integration,[19] faculty play a primary role in helping students assimilate both an institution's academic norms and values as well as its social climate. Particularly at campuses with high percentages of commuter students, the faculty role in both academic and social integration of students into the campus culture is key. Generally, the only opportunity for nontraditional students—older than the traditional 18- to 24-year-old cohort, enrolled part time, academically underprepared, living off-campus, and working at least 20 hours a week, or with family responsibilities—to assimilate institutional values and norms is in the classroom. None of the two-year campuses—approximately 41 percent of the higher education enrollment mix in Maryland in 1994—has residential facilities.[20]

Generally, an institution's senior faculty have more teaching, research, and administrative experience than junior faculty members. Research found that more contact with faculty enhances the quality of the learning environment for students at colleges and universities. One could argue that more contact with senior faculty may enhance the quality of the learning environment for students more than contact with junior faculty precisely because senior faculty members have more teaching, research, and administrative experience. In *The Condition of Education*, data show that at research, doctoral, and comprehensive institutions in both 1987 and 1992, the majority of classroom exposure to faculty for students in undergraduate upper-division courses and graduate courses was with senior faculty: full professors and associate professors. At comprehensive institutions in 1992, undergraduate students in lower-division courses had less classroom exposure to senior faculty than students in upper-division courses. Students in undergraduate courses at research institutions had about the same classroom exposure to senior-level faculty as students in undergraduate courses at comprehensive and liberal arts institutions. However, undergraduates in classes taught by senior-level faculty at research institutions were more likely to be in classes of more than 50 students than their counterparts at comprehensive and liberal arts institutions.

Institutional policy to enhance student success is an important area of study for colleges and universities. At too many institutions, there is an overreliance on contractual instructors for teaching first- and second-year students. In many cases this is the result of flat to declining state appropriations to higher education and increases in enrollment. For example, the Maryland Higher Education Commission, recognizing the need for quality in undergraduate education, provided in its "Minimum Requirements for Degree-Granting Institutions" that full-time faculty teach at least 50 percent of the instruction for which credits toward degrees are awarded.[21] However, because the standard is applied institutionwide, at some institutions this means that certain programs are taught mostly by part-time faculty. At the institutional level, senior administrators and faculty should work to reduce the relatively high number of part-time and/or contractual instructors teaching first- and second-year students. The quality of instruction during the first two years of college—particularly the first year—is crucial to establishing the student-faculty interactions that help students establish lifelong educational goals and assimilate specific institutional values.

Another priority of senior administrators and faculty should be organized incentives and opportunities for developmental activities centered around classroom research on improving teaching. Examples may include applied research on the use of learning technologies and student achievement and other pedagogies for varied student groups such as learning communities. Actively involving students in learning has been documented to improve student achievement at the K–12 level and increasingly with significant numbers of nontraditional students and students of color at urban commuter campuses. Especially at institutions other than research universities, faculty responsibilities should include participation in field experiences and applied research that involves working with K–12 teachers and peers at community colleges.

Learning communities are one teaching/learning practice that encourages student and teacher involvement and retention. A learning community is often pairs or clusters of courses that faculty plan together so that the content in one course reinforces the content in the others. Students often work in groups. Often, faculty choose to team teach linked courses and thus have to collaborate. The method provides opportunities to renew faculty, and it challenges colleagues—some tenured and some not—from across disciplines to work together and to employ different presentation approaches. General education and core program planners are turning to learning communities to accomplish for students the kind of holistic experience that taking separate courses can't provide. Evergreen State University (Wash.) and Portland State University (Ore.) have experienced much success with their implementation of campus-specific versions of learning communities. Dillard University (La.) and LaGuardia Community College (N.Y.) have found that learning communities are a useful model with diversely prepared students. Faculty should be recognized and rewarded for implementing varied pedagogical models and for documenting their effectiveness. Rewards could include campus mini-grants and funds to travel to conferences to present their classroom research papers and to share lessons learned with colleagues from various types of institutions.

Similar to the recent emphasis in student retention literature on the role of faculty involvement, K–12 researchers have begun to call for a re-examination of teacher education and teacher training, recognizing that teachers play a critical role in shaping children's career expectations and attitudes about learning. When students come to college ill prepared, keeping them in school becomes a greater challenge. The U.S. Department of Education reported that 78 percent of higher education institutions that enrolled college freshmen in 1995 offered at least one remedial reading, writing, or mathematics course.[22] The Maryland Higher Education Commission surveyed all public two- and four-year institutions in the state and found that 90 percent of all remedial education is offered at community colleges, versus 10 percent at four-year comprehensive/liberal arts campuses. Furthermore, 47 percent of all new students at Maryland public institutions who enrolled directly from high school needed some form of remediation. The trend was most evident at community colleges and institutions with a significant number of minority students.[23]

Conclusion

Researchers agree on exemplary practices and policies that facilitate student success. Almost all experts agree that retention programs need to be part of a campus-wide retention effort and not an isolated add-on program for special students. Unfortunately, campus administrators have been reluctant to engage faculty in these campus-wide efforts. Instead, student development and academic support staff have been delegated the tasks of addressing those social and academic variables that affect whether students stay in or leave college. Campuses also have been slow to adopt the principles of planned change when it comes to problem-solving focused on improving student retention and graduation rates. Few practitioners want to invest the time and effort to identify and involve experts on campus in eliminating the barriers to increased student retention and graduation rates by using data collection tools and solution planning and implementation. Even student retention programs with documented successful outcomes rarely undergo formative evaluations so they might improve and be integrated into campus-wide goals.

Looking at the efforts of one state, this author finds that the results are not always immediate. For example, while Maryland has made considerable progress toward realizing parity in the retention and graduation rates of majority and minority students, a gap still persists between the six-year graduation rates of minority (39.4 percent) and majority (64.7 percent) students. The gap in graduation rates of community college transfer students who are African American (30 percent) and white (52 percent) remained basically unchanged for the past five cohorts.

Maryland legislators have served as catalysts for change in student retention practices and policies; initially, they focused on retention and graduation rates at the state's four historically black institutions. Further, as part of the state's performance accountability process, the Maryland Higher Education Commission now requires public colleges and universities to prepare a minority achievement plan and annual progress reports which focus on the retention, transfer, and graduation patterns of minority students. The reports contain analyses of trends in retention and graduation rates and a discussion of institutional activities that have improved student retention, including efforts in the areas of academic advising, personal counseling, developmental education, and extracurricular planning.

In *A Conceptual Framework for Student Retention in Science, Engineering, and Mathematics Programs*, Swail asks the following questions in reference to teaching and learning practices and student success: What is the role of faculty in the development of an effective institutionwide student retention program? What policies are needed to support curriculum revision? What policies are needed to support the development of better teaching practices? What policies are needed to support the administrative and organizational changes involved in the institutionwide retention program?

Richardson encourages campuses to address these questions via campus studies. Based on his case study data, only when campuses try to tackle these tough questions will they start to see improvements in graduation rates. Certainly the Pew Charitable Trusts agrees. By honoring colleges for their efforts to improve undergraduate education, Pew provides tangible recognition ($250,000) to up to five schools annually that have "broken out of the box of familiar structures"[24] to make fundamental changes in their teaching and learning processes.

What do these institutions and others that promulgate best practices in teaching and learning have in common? Typically, these institutions have involved faculty and administrators in the development of positive learning environments and have campus cultures that emphasize high standards of teaching and learning, faculty as role models and mentors to students, faculty active in the advisement and freshman orientation programs, faculty active in classroom research and varied pedagogical practices, and staff and students who provide necessary academic and social support services.

National data point to the lack of preparedness of a significant percentage of students to pursue college-level studies. In Maryland, research shows that African American students who take college preparatory courses, particularly in math and

English, are less likely to require remedial assistance than students who do not take college preparatory classes in high school.[25] There appears to be a positive correlation between the academic preparedness variable and student persistence.

As attacks on affirmative action increase, specifically race preferences in admissions, colleges and universities are targeting programs at the middle schools and high schools that aim to prepare minority youths for higher standards in mathematics and science by steering them toward competitive college preparatory curricula, even in vocationally oriented school-to-work programs. This appears to be the model for the future. Collaboration between K–16 teachers/faculty and administrators on teaching and learning practices (particularly at the high school level) that will ensure student success at the postsecondary level, from occupational and technical career choices to more traditional college majors, supports this model. Typically, this model also involves the business community as a catalyst for higher standards and support of ongoing professional development for teachers and faculty. Attention given to higher standards must also take into account the need to remain inclusive. At the state policy level, this means attention to both access and quality.

Notes

[1]Maryland Higher Education Commission. *A Study of Remedial Education at Maryland Public Campuses*, May 1996.

[2]SHEEO/NCES Communication Network News, Vol. 15, No. 3, December 1996, pp. 2–5.

[3]Carter, Deborah J., and Reginald Wilson. *Annual Status Report on Minorities in Higher Education: 1994*. Washington, DC; American Council on Education 1995, pp. 2–9.

[4]Maryland Higher Education Commission. *A Study of the Workforce Needs of Maryland Employers*, September 1996.

[5]U.S. Department of Education. *The Condition of Education 1995*. Washington, DC: National Center for Education Statistics 1995, p. vi.

[6]Ibid., p. 25.

[7]Ibid.

[8]Ibid., p. vi.

[9]To attend college on a full-time basis, however, requires that the student pay tuition costs and living expenses, as well (ibid., p. vii.).

[10]Ibid., p. 25.

[11]U.S. Department of Education. National Center for Education Statistics. *The Condition of Education 1996*, NCES 96-304. Washington, DC: U.S. Government Printing Officer, 1996, p. 58.

[12]Ibid., p. 58

[13]Ibid., p. 92.

[14]Ibid., p.144.

[15]Tinto, Vincent. *Leaving College*. Chicago: University of Chicago Press, 1987.

[16]Astin, Alexander W. *Minorities in Higher Education*. San Francisco: Jossey-Bass Publishers, 1982.

[17]U. S. Department of Education. National Center for Education Statistics. *Minority Undergraduate Participation in Postsecondary Education*, NCES 95-166. Washington, DC: U.S. Government Printing Office, 1995, p. iii.

[18]Richardson, Richard C. Jr., and E. F. Skinner. *Achieving Quality and Diversity*. New York: Washington, DC: ACE/Macmillan, 1991.

[19]Tinto, op. cit., 1987.

[20]Maryland Higher Education Commission, *Data Book*, 1997.

[21]Annotated Code of Maryland (1992 Replacement Volume and 1996 Supplement), Maryland Higher Education Commission.

[22]U.S. Department of Education. *Remedial Education at Higher Education Institutions in Fall 1995*. National Center for Education Statistics, October 1996.

[23]Maryland Higher Education Commission. *A Study of Remedial Education at Maryland Public Campuses*. May 1996.

[24]Maryland Higher Education Commission *Relationship Between High School and College Performance by Maryland Students*, November 1996.

Bibliography

Astin, A. *Minorities in Higher Education*. San Francisco: Jossey-Bass Publishers, 1982.

Carter, D. and R. Wilson. *Annual Status Report on Minorities in Higher Education, 1994*. Washington, DC: American Council on Education 1995, pp. 2–9.

Maryland Higher Education Commission. *A Study of Remedial Education at Maryland Public Campuses*, May 1996.

Maryland Higher Education Commission. *A Study of the Workforce Needs of Maryland Employers*, September 1996.

Maryland Higher Education Commission, *Data Book*, 1997.

Maryland Higher Education Commission. *Relationship Between High School and College Performance by Maryland Students*, November 1996.

Frederick D. Patterson Research Institute of The College Fund/UNCF. *The African American Education Data Book Volume I: Higher and Adult Education* by Michael T. Nettles and Laura W. Perna. Fairfax, VA, 1997.

Richardson, R. C. Jr. and E. Skinner. *Achieving Quality and Diversity*. Washington, DC: ACE/Macmillan, 1991.

SHEEO/NCES Communication Network News, Vol. 15, No. 3, December 1996: pp. 2–5.

Swail, S. *A Conceptual Framework for Student Retention in Science, Engineering, and Mathematics Programs*. Unpublished doctoral dissertation, George Washington University, Washington, DC, 1995.

Tinto, V. *Leaving College*. Chicago: University of Chicago Press, 1987.

U.S. Department of Education. National Center for Education Statistics. *The Condition of Education,1996*, NCES 96-304, by Thomas M. Smith. Washington, DC: U.S. Government Printing Office, 1996.

U.S. Department of Education. National Center for Education Statistics. *Minority Undergraduate Participation in Postsecondary Education*, NCES 95-166, by Laura Horn and Carlyle Maw. Washington, DC: U.S. Government Printing Office, 1995.

From Shifting Sands to Bedrock: Equity as Excellence via Pedagogical Pluralism

Joel M. Jones
President
Fort Lewis College

"We've tried affirmative action for 30 years and it hasn't worked, so let's get off that horse," pronounced the cab driver taking me back to the airport from One Dupont Circle. Only a sophomoric novelist could have scripted this scenario and the unfolding conversation. Having just spent most of the day with a small group of colleagues from higher education convened by the American Association of State Colleges and Universities to discuss "life after affirmative action," I listened to this cab driver (a community college graduate) pointedly and poignantly substantiate all of the concerns we had about the cultural backlash, political retrogression, and legal retreat regarding affirmative action. Our focus in this essay will not be a discussion of whether or not affirmative action has worked. Obviously, for some individuals on many campuses the process has worked quite well, while for many others, the affirmative action process has been simply that: a process with no meaningful results.

Perhaps the best succinct statement on the several perversities and paradoxes of affirmative action was made recently by my colleague, Al Yates: "Rather than bringing people of different races and cultures together in an atmosphere of respect and understanding, there is now a clear sense that affirmative action has contributed to polarization and growing hostility among disparate groups." Yates, as one of the most successful black scholars and presidents in the country, has had to deal with individuals who would assume both that he had benefited from affirmative action and that he would be an automatic champion thereof. His abilities and his accomplishments (for those of us who know him) have nothing to do with his ethnicity. His perspective on this topic, therefore, carries weight. Yates continues:

> Too many Americans feel threatened or betrayed by affirmative action as it now exists; too many others fear the important benefits of affirmative action are outweighed by the stigma that has been attached to it. Our challenge today is to look at the issue from a fresh perspective and to craft new and constructive ways to level the playing field, to open our country's opportunities to all citizens without closing off opportunity to any.[2]

Our focus here will be to explore the ways by which our campuses, as dynamic educational communities, can continue to identify, address, and enhance the learning potential and opportunity for the educational maturation of every individual who becomes part of the campus community. From entry to exit, much of what we would do as educators remains mysterious, even magical, while momentous in terms of both individual and societal impact. Mysterious, magical, momentous—but, now by necessity, for those of us working in the public educational arena, measurable in terms of our respective institutional missions. A fundamental measure of our success will be our ability to incorporate diversity and pedagogical pluralism into our mission statements—and to hold ourselves accountable for proffering an educational environment both engaging and elevating to our students, regardless of their ethnicity, gender, age, socioeconomic background, or physical abilities.

When I was asked if I would contribute to this new AASCU publication, the editor commented, "Under access and diversity issues that have an impact on retention, we want you to cover race-based scholarships, integration versus multiculturalism or individualism, the inclusive university, and community-building." Then, with classic understatement, noting that though this "would be fodder for an entire book," she asked that I see this essay more "as a 'how-to' manual" than an extended philosophical treatise. So, we will do our best to move through the shifting sands of philosophical and political discourse in quest of more specific programmatic directives, recognizing always that in academia the two are never separate—especially when the means and the end (as articulated in this essay) will be "pedagogical pluralism."

My initial caveat must be this: I am still struggling after 30 years in higher education as a professor and administrator (and ten years on my current campus as president) to identify and initiate the best ways to promote and protect pluralism and diversity, especially given the particularities of the people and place which constitute any campus community. Therefore, it would be presumptuous to delineate a list of "how-tos" which would be universally applicable to all campuses. Also, the quest for applicable programs and projects will move through philosophy, campus politics, and pedagogy and will weave a fabric of many beginnings with only brief spots of momentary closure.

Having been professionally committed to "cultural pluralism" for more than 30 years, I want desperately to find a new hook upon which to posit this essay, a new angle by which to engage the reader's attention, a blazing insight by which to cut through all the rhetoric and miasmic mist which surrounds so many of these conversations—and I anguish at the recognition that most of the individuals who will take the time to read this new AASCU publication and to work with the ideas contained herein will be the "converted," those individuals who already believe in the inherent relationship between equity and excellence, access and achievement, individual meaning and community connections, pluralism and progress.

First, we must remember when speaking about "retention" and "graduation" that one student's continuing retention could be another student's version of incarceration. We all, as educators, must recognize that in fact there is no correlation between simply staying in school, graduating, and what we would value most about the educational process. Moreover, speaking from the vantage point of an institution which has as one of its historical missions the education of Native American students, to insist on retention (continuous enrollment) as a measure of success could run directly contrary to much more important values (e.g., family loyalty) which some of our students bring with them to campus. I share that simply by way of noting that we must all decide, in terms of the specific mission and nature of our respective campuses, how we would best articulate "success" with reference to the traditional definitions of "retention" and "graduation rate."

There are so many good proposals and projects in place, well defined and written up in easily accessible formats, that one hesitates to take more time and space to reinvent wheels and spin them. I would suggest that anyone really committed to the issue of attracting, retaining, and graduating students of any type should read Vince Tinto's *Leaving College: Rethinking the Causes and Cures of Student Attrition*. Professor Tinto and his colleagues have spent years studying the specific issue of retention and graduation (or, from the other perspective, attrition), and his work should be at the core of any institution's thinking about these issues.

In fact, I would suggest that we all need to find a way to encourage our faculty and staff to read more of the exponentially burgeoning literature about higher education. We all have been in too many conversations on too many campuses (in my own experience ranging from large research universities to small private colleges) where faculty and staff sitting at the table have been either too busy or too disinterested to be familiar with the work of Astin, Boyer, Chickering, and Cross, or any of the others who have taken the time to research carefully the processes which characterize the educational experience at our institutions. How do we get our non-committed colleagues on campus (and there are many) to read and take seriously this literature? Correlatively, how do we get the members of our governing boards and their colleagues in positions of political and economic influence to read this literature and take it to heart and mind? How? Perhaps by simply continuing to stress the fact that our nation has changed, that old academic ways and ideas will no longer work (if they ever did), and that if our world is not only to survive but to improve, we must light the moral and ethical fires which will illuminate the interconnectedness and viability of multiple values and visions we encounter as we move through the course of an educational day. We need, of course, to preach a little—but we must practice a lot.

On our campus, for example, a teaching-intensive public liberal arts college, we have dedicated monies for several years to specific faculty and staff development projects which pertain to pluralism and diversity. In addition to sending groups of our faculty and staff to workshops and conferences (asking them to share their learning with the rest of their colleagues upon returning), I have seen it as one of my roles to simply purchase and distribute books and monographs of specific interest (including many of the items on the attached bibliography) to many members of our campus community.

Having already initiated several entries into this essay, let me begin another—since, as one might realize, an essay which purports to deal with transforming campuses into learning environments of diverse peoples and diverse learning styles must stylistically reflect its substantive message: this transformative process, a series of continuous beginnings, will never be finished or completed. The best one can do is to initiate new procedures, new measures, new programs on a fairly regular basis (not a common practice in academia) to accommodate the changing complexion and complexity of the student population. Some of these initiatives, some of these beginnings, will prove to be more effective, more successful, than others. Those, of course, we should sustain through their period of efficacy. Others may prove to have been well-intended efforts but off the mark. For those, we should simply move beyond our personal and programmatic invested interests, either making the appropriate accommodations or starting from scratch with reference to a particular pedagogical principle in response to a student-group need. Metaphorically, we might talk about these efforts as shifting sands which must become the bedrock of a given student's learning experience. This sounds challenging, but it can work.

As a white male administrator (one whose primary work in cultural diversity has been with Hispanic and Native American students in the southwestern United States), let me practice what I would preach (moving outside the realm of my daily contacts) and use the words of three black spokespersons to dramatize the view we must promote in order to awaken many of those around us. In concluding his collection of essays, *The Crisis of Color and Democracy: Essays on Race, Class, and Power*, Manning Marable comments:

> The next half century will be a transition from a white majority society
> to a society which is far more pluralistic and diverse, where multilin-
> gualism is increasingly the norm, where different cultures, religions,

and philosophies are a beautiful mosaic of human exchange and inter-action. *That* is the emerging majority.[3]

Many of us live where the demographics have already demonstrated the validity of Dr. Marable's vision. Many of us also live and work with individuals who simply continue to deny the validity and viability of that vision—contrary to what they experience in the world around them. The strains of racism, sexism, homophobia, anti-environmental insensitivity, and discrimination against the disabled all run deep in the core of our common culture. (Note: Our programmatic commitment was to bring Dr. Marable to our southwestern campus two years ago as the keynote speaker for our year-long series of activities and workshops on diversity. His voice, to our audience, was new and strong.)

Accepting the reality of Marable's view of the future, we might move further beyond the legal definition of "affirmative action" by looking at statements by two other black scholars. First, in her brilliant work, *The Alchemy of Race and Rights*, Patricia Williams writes:

> It is thus that affirmative action is an affirmation; the affirmative act of hiring—or hearing—blacks is a recognition of individuality that re-places blacks as a social statistic, that is profoundly interconnective to the fate of blacks and whites either as subgroups or as one group. In this sense, affirmative action is as mystical and beyond-the-self as an initiation ceremony. It is an act of verification and of vision. It is an act of social as well as professional responsibility.[4]

To a professional (in this case, an accomplished lawyer) like Patricia Williams, affirmative action has meant so much—and yet, quite quickly, given current legal interpretations, it may come to mean so little to many others.

Echoing that concern would be the voice of Cornel West in *Race Matters*. He proclaims:

> Progressives should view affirmative action as neither a major solution to poverty nor a sufficient means to equality. We should see it as prima-rily playing a negative role—namely, to ensure that discriminatory prac-

tices against women and people of color are abated. Given the history of this country, it is a virtual certainty that without affirmative action, racial and sexual discrimination would return with a vengeance.[5]

We would like to believe that Professor West has overstated the negative possibility. However, given the escalating legal retreat from affirmative action, I fear the validity of his prognosis. Therefore, we have no choice but simply to move beyond the legal recourse to affirmative action and develop moral, ethical, and pedagogical principles which we must integrate with the fundamental missions and mandates of our respective institutions. The issue of race-based scholarships, for example, can be transcended by moving to multiple admissions criteria which will provide a diverse learning community (first-generation, socioeconomic status, as well as gender and ethnicity), a community predicated upon a commitment to the principles of pedagogical pluralism.

We are, in fact, I hope, still engaged in what is defined as a form of "higher" education—and, in this context, that designation of "higher" must refer to the principles and practices by which we would define our daily work. Morality, ethics, and value-laden principles must become both form and function of our daily discourse. Otherwise, we will allow ourselves to be driven simply by "efficiency" and "efficacy" measured only in *economic* terms.

In a world in which the commitment to access to higher education has been seriously undermined, we must realize that to focus attention on retention and graduation rates will become a futile exercise if we allow other factors to force us to shut our doors to those who both need us most and have the most to bring to our educational communities by way of broadening our perspective on the world. Analyses such as Paul Lauter's may seem extreme if read during a "good day" on any of our campuses. However, when one reads his well-documented description of the deliberate retreat from access to higher education in *Higher Education Under Fire: Politics, Economics, and the Crisis of the Humanities*, one realizes that we simply cannot sit back and let "nature take its course," or "the marketplace play out." To do so means we will see a chauvinistic and nostalgic resurgence of an elitist and exclusive view of higher education, a view which still governs the thinking of too many commentators. After convincingly documenting the economic "hit" which public institutions of higher education (such as many of our AASCU institutions) have taken over the past decade, Lauter issues the following challenge:

> Those of us who are committed to broadening educational access and who believe in the value of multiculturalism and sex and gender equity need, I believe, to persuade Americans, as we have not successfully done, of the value of what we and our students do in colleges and universities. Many people have become skeptical of that enterprise, and indeed, in traditional American fashion, of intellectual work generally. In fact, one might argue that the real crisis of higher education has to do with the sharp decline of its authority, most particularly its cultural authority.[6]

With that challenge in mind, I would reiterate my insistence that we find a way to expose our own faculty and staff to the well-reasoned and well-documented research of Astin, Boyer, Chickering, Cross, and others—that research which demonstrates so convincingly the value of diversity, multiculturalism, cultural pluralism (pick your term) with reference to the moral and ethical maturation of the students on our campuses.

On our campus at Fort Lewis College in Durango, Colorado, we have tried to move multicultural content to the center of our core curriculum; we have encouraged and funded the participation of many of our faculty members in cultural awareness training; we have initiated myriad programs in student services to enhance appreciation and understanding of diverse ways of seeing-thinking-living-learning; we have struggled to make our faculty and staff more reflective of the diversity of our region (still our most marginal area of accomplishment); and we have put in place several federally funded programs (through the Fund for the Improvement of Postsecondary Education, the National Endowment for the Humanities, and the National Science Foundation) and privately funded programs (more than $3 million from the Hughes Biomedical Foundation) which will bring our students (and especially students of color and disability) closer to that sense of "engagement" and "interaction" and "involvement" with their educational experience which Vince Tinto's research documents as so critical to retention and educational maturation.

All of us, though, must acknowledge daily that racism, sexism, homophobia, disrespect for the environment, crass materialism, and solipsistic self-indulgence run rampant in our national culture—and are reflected daily in many ways on our respective campuses. We cannot rest on our laurels—be those laurels statistics from the EEO office or data provided to board members and legislators showing that we are improving in the recruitment, retention, and graduation of students of color and women. Most of us, in fact, have only scratched the surface, have only begun to develop the consciousness and conscience which would characterize communities of trust and civil discourse.

To build community one needs to establish trust. To establish trust (always a complicated and continuing process), one might suggest the following ABCDs: *acknowledge* the ambivalence and ambiguity attendant upon any truly significant decision; *balance* the varying participating perspectives from diverse communities and the values attendant upon those perspectives; *clarify* the connections among those diverse perspectives, the connections both causal and consequential; and then *decide*—knowing that very few decisions will garner universal applause or accolades, but hoping that all constituencies will understand why and how the decision was made and that their voice was both heard and honored.

Ernest Boyer addressed these issues in two works. In the first, *College: The Undergraduate Experience in America*, Boyer outlined the problems characterizing undergraduate education in America: the accumulation of information versus the formation of the individual; individual needs versus community commitments; and the affirmation of diversity versus the exploration of commonalities.[7] According to Boyer, academics need to realize that these processes neither conflict with nor contradict each other. Rather, they constitute a synergistic dynamic, the basis for both cognitive and affective individual growth and community consciousness. Boyer expanded his analysis in the Carnegie report, *Campus Life: In Search of Community*. He proposed in dramatic terms a commitment to community as the solution to the aforementioned curricular conflicts and academic ambivalence.[8] Boyer expressed a perspective in *Campus Life* that should be the basis not only for our thinking on equity and excellence, diversity and community, but for classroom discourse and the campus ethos in general:

We believe that standards of communication, especially on a college campus, must go far beyond correct grammar or syntax; they even must extend beyond the "civility" of the message being sent. A higher standard is to view communication as a "sacred trust." The goal of human discourse must be to both speak and listen with great care and seek understanding at the deepest level, and this expectation takes on special significance as the nation's campuses become increasingly diverse.[9]

We were so moved by the poignancy of this call by Boyer that we entitled a new history of our college, *Sacred Trust: The Birth and Development of Fort Lewis College*. Whether we choose to discuss the issue of demographics and diversity, the democratic ideal versus the elitist ethos in the liberal arts tradition, the need for a network of small learning communities or ethnic enclaves in the world of mass education and megalopolis multiversities, we must pay heed to Boyer's focus on communication as a sacred trust. We must be able to live and learn in a community where we are free to speak and be heard with integrity. The academic community must value the vision and voice of each individual, while seeking and shaping coherence and continuity from the seemingly chaotic chorus of the collective voices. Open communication must become a primary commitment as both a means and an end to efforts in higher education. With such a commitment there would be no need for campus codes for discourse and dialogue; each member of the community would see in the other a resource for personal enlightenment and enrichment. Our very diversity would become a tool for true intellectual and spiritual growth, a far better measure of excellence in our pluralistic global community.

By way of another beginning, the request to discuss the future of "cultural diversity" or "cultural pluralism" on campuses "after affirmative action" presents several dilemmas. First, we need always to acknowledge the moral, ethical, and pedagogical imperative for promoting and protecting cultural diversity and cultural pluralism on our campuses. The literature supporting that point of view now proffers overwhelming research evidence (regarding the educational benefits of a diverse campus) and programmatic models for our purview. At our respective institutions, we must reflect honestly on the problems we face, the progress we have made to date, and the programs we need to implement, given our answers to the first two questions. We really don't need more verbiage on this topic; we simply need more vision, more courage, and more commitment. To presidents, I would say, assess yourself, then your cabinet, then your colleagues on the faculty and staff, and then the general climate of opinion when all of those attitudes are mixed with those of your current student body; then plant the seeds for and nurture programmatic initiatives.

Fortunately, substantial literature on this topic has been generated by many higher education associations, such as the American Association of State Colleges and Universities, the Western Interstate Commission for Higher Education, the American Council on Education, The College Board, and the Education Commission of the States (see the bibliography that follows this essay). These groups have produced many publications that corroborate the integral link between access and achievement, equity and excellence. A statement by Richard Richardson, Jr. and Alfredo de los Santos, both of whom have done very good work in this area, embodies the substance and spirit of these publications:

> In the past it has been common to define quality in higher education as a function of those excluded. Those excluded were disproportionately minority. Today, most people believe that any workable definition of quality must accommodate diversity. Such accommodation need not be at the expense of rigor and excellence. Minority students need a high-quality education if degrees are to mean anything for anyone.[10]

This call for access and achievement, equity and excellence, has been issued by many authors.[11] Among the many, several statements crystallize key issues and conclusions:

- Without quality in education, the nation loses its strength. Without equity in education, democracy ceases to function. ... True educational excellence ... is not possible without true educational equity.[12]

- I came to realize that the issue of equity versus excellence is really more a matter of how we define excellence ... [and] it appears that the quest for excellence has been given much higher priority than the issue of equal access.[13]

- The roots of inequality remain deeply embedded in the structure of a higher education system that is scientifically mature and socially immature.[14]

Regardless of the definition of diversity by which we would measure the success of our campus (by ethnicity, gender, age, environmental attitude, sexual preference, or whether they are differently abled, nontraditional, or any other descriptor that might carry with it a particular value orientation, though such correlation always runs the risk of stereotyping), we must realize that the process of initiating and implementing new programs reflective of authentic pedagogical pluralism will engage us in a process of many beginnings with only momentary closure.

As each of us enters any campus learning community, we bring with us our idiosyncrasies as learners with our individual learning abilities or (if you will) learning disabilities, consequences of nature (heredity) or nurturance (early home or learning environments)—each of which will condition or influence the nature of our participation and success (or failure) in the learning community. All one needs to do is to read either Howard Gardner (*Multiple Intelligences*) or Daniel Goleman (*Emotional Intelligence*) to realize the viability and validity of this statement—and the dramatic changes it should call for in most of our pedagogical approaches, regardless of the current nature of the learning community. This challenge is what we would encompass under the term "pedagogical pluralism"—and why we would insist that any conversation about "diversity" or "cultural pluralism" on a campus must incorporate these new understandings in the psychology and philosophy of education if, in fact, we intend to establish diverse learning communities that are engaging, exciting, and truly educational. The successes in these "value-added" learning communities are measurable, though not always quantifiable in simplistic numerical terms, and should be incorporated into the mission statements of our respective campus communities.

In *Achieving Quality and Diversity: Universities in a Multicultural Society*, Richard Richardson Jr. and Elizabeth Skinner provide in-depth descriptions of integrative campus climates at ten institutions. Obviously, no perfect campus strategy or scenario exists, but some have succeeded more than most at expanding access while enhancing achievement. Richardson and Skinner placed their study in the context of one rather perplexing paradox of contemporary American higher education: "Quite clearly, colleges and universities have served in the last quarter century both as promoters of upward mobility and as defenders of prevailing social privilege."[15] However, their statistics, success stories, and three stages of campus maturation—reactive, strategic, adaptive—assist all of us who acknowledge that significant success, the sustained synergy of access and achievement, requires "fundamental changes in institutional practices and priorities."[16] According to Ernest Boyer, to initiate and implement the requisite changes in our teaching and research epistemology, in the ethic of our policies and programs, will demand, "a moment for boldness in higher education."[17]

In one of the bolder educational treatises of late, *Teaching to Transgress: Education as the Practice of Freedom*, Bell Hooks provides an engaging and enlightening contemporary testimonial on the connection between pedagogy, politics, and pluralism, stressing emphatically the role of community building as a liberating art. Ms. Hooks notes that "as a teacher in the classroom," she has "witnessed the power of a transformative pedagogy rooted in a respect for multiculturalism."[18] She says we must "enter the classroom with the assumption that we must build 'community' in order to create a climate of openness and intellectual rigor."[19] New materials alone will not produce a multicultural classroom, Hooks warns feminists and ethnic educators, as well as the still prevalent traditionalists. As changing demographics dictate a diversity of learning styles in nearly all collegiate classrooms, many of us, according to Hooks, being "poorly prepared . . . [to] actually confront diversity . . . will stubbornly cling to old patterns"[20] of authoritarian pedagogy. If we listen, we will enable all our students "to recognize the value of each individual voice," then we will link, says Hooks, our "ways of knowing with habits of being,"[21] and we will experience community building as an ethical framework for our new epistemology.

As I wrote several years ago—and still believe passionately:

> Faculty, students, staff, and administrators need to bring mind and heart, intellect and intuition, precision and passion, energies calculative and creative, to our daily classroom encounters, campus conversations, and community activities. Recognizing that the circle of learning never closes and that the community of learners is never fully realized, we must live to love to learn together.[22]

Questions from the front . . .

Q. How can you promote diversity on a large campus (20K plus) with a small African American population as well as small minority ethnic groups where the majority faculty doesn't see the need for diversity?

A. I would suggest that the best approach to a faculty which "doesn't see the need for diversity" in this day and age might range from bringing in speakers from the outside who reflect in their experience the truly multicultural and diverse nature of contemporary society, to sending members of the faculty leadership to the many meetings and workshops sponsored nationwide by all of the higher education associations with the mandate that these faculty will return to campus and share their thoughts with their colleagues. Moreover, one can most appropriately refer to the conversation in this essay about the relationship between pedagogy and pluralism with reference to the extant evidence about learning styles and learning environments most appropriate for individual and collective maturation.

Q. Who is the "minority" student?

A. For a variety of reasons, we should move beyond the old descriptor "minority." First of all, there are those of us who live in regions (for example, the Southwest) where the demographics have changed so dramatically, both on campus and in the surrounding communities, that students of color may well be (at least in number) the majority student. Again, I would suggest that using the pedagogical rationale for addressing diverse learning styles will transcend the now dated approach to the definition of a "minority" student. At some moment, each of us becomes a minority of one hoping that someone will acknowledge and respond to our individual potential and personal learning style—and that in so responding, they will strengthen the fabric of the community in which we would learn, live, work, and play.

Q. Are disabled students considered a minority? They face the same discriminations and educational challenges, yet when we speak of diversity and multiculturalism, that population of students is almost never addressed. Please comment.

A. I would note that both the substance and tone of this question ring true to my own experience. That is, having participated in numerous workshops and conferences on "diversity" issues, it seems too often that issues pertaining to "disabled students" (or, as one might better say it, differently abled students), are addressed as an afterthought or as parenthetical to what are seen as the fundamental issues of racism, sexism, and gender preference. Such should not be the case. Though our campus was no further ahead on this curve than most a decade ago, we have made measurable progress in addressing Americans with Disabilities Act (ADA) requirements and, in general, in making our campus more accommodating and manageable for students with different disabilities. In fact, during the past several years, some of those students in wheel chairs, or blind, or with a hearing disability have emerged as outstanding students and student leaders as measured by any standards. Significant federal monies have been made available in most states—and if an institution has taken the initiative to put a well-articulated plan in place, those monies have been quickly and readily available. On our campus, leadership in that role has been exercised by our vice president for business and finance, an individual who experienced polio at the age of eighteen, leaving him paraplegic, but motivating him to be a hyper-achiever in the academic arena. His commitment has allowed our campus to take the lead in transforming ourselves into a hospitable environment for students with all kinds of "disabilities" (or, preferably, differently focused abilities).

Q. **As a white male professor, is there a danger that I may "overstep" my bounds in encouraging minority development and fellowship/scholarship applications?**

A. Quite simply, no. Go for it. We need leadership from "white male professors" in this arena, leadership based on understanding and empathy, not on guilt and sympathy. If there is any risk on your campus, take it. Helping your campus transform itself into a truly "diverse" learning environment can prove to be the most meaningful dimension of one's academic career.

Q. **In communication, values as well as language are important. Are there resources that could help college personnel deepen their understanding and appreciation of different values?**

A. Absolutely. First, see Pamela Arrington's review in this book of the literature on diversity and multiculturalism. Moreover, numerous workshops and conferences are available to any faculty or staff person with an interest in broadening one's perspective on values and language. If your budget has strict limitations, as is too often the case (especially with public institutions these days), much can be accessed through the publications listed in this book. In addition, as a former professor of literature, I would hasten to add that an extraordinary education can be had with reference to values and language just through exposure to appropriate fiction. For example, I would hope that anyone teaching in the southwestern United States would be familiar with the novels and essays of Rudolfo Anaya, Leslie Silko, or Simon Ortiz, to name just three of the many writers one could cite as having either Native American or Hispanic roots.

Q. **As a minority who attended a predominantly white institution, I believe it is imperative that there be mandatory sensitivity training for faculty and students on an ongoing basis. I agree that it is very important to have diverse student populations at colleges and universities, but I would urge faculty members to refrain from soliciting one student's viewpoint as representative of his entire race!**

A. Yes, in the context of a classroom conversation, "one student's viewpoint" should reflect only the position and perspective of that student, should be solicited only in that context, and should be discussed only in that way. With reference to the first concern in this statement—"Mandatory sensitivity training for faculty and students,": As an individual whose personal pedagogy and educational philosophy for more than 30 years has had a problem linking "mandatory" with "educational," I am continually challenged by how we best get beyond working with the converted (or preaching to the choir) and find ways to broaden the perspective of faculty members or students who seem locked in time by their biases or prejudices. All one can do is discuss approaches taken at other campuses (for example, we have been engaged now for two years, with limited success, with a voluntary project focused on faculty and classroom relationships) and see how other programs might be adapted (either as voluntary or mandatory) to fit the spirit and soul, the "culture," of your respective campus.

Q. **How do you get people involved who do not want to be involved but who "need" to be involved if there is truly going to be a change in "institutional" thinking?**

A. See my response to the preceding question—and especially my pointed ambiguity about mandating programs in diversity training. Somehow, with continuing commitment and struggle, we need to change the culture of our institutions to reflect a commitment to pedagogical pluralism. If we can get our faculty and staff to acknowledge the documentable fact that we all learn and grow in different ways, then I believe we can get all of our campus players to understand the need for their own continual growth and development with reference to their own skills in pedagogy and interpersonal communication.

Q. **Understanding differences is going to require honest debate: How do we balance the cathartic nature of debate with political correctness?**

A. First, as I discuss in the preceding essay (and have expanded on in an essay published earlier this year—see "The Liberal Art of Community Building: From Aristotle to Anaya, Socrates to Silko"), I believe that campuses have always been "politically correct"; the politics have simply changed. More important, using Ernest Boyer's terminology, I do believe that the "sacred trust" of our campuses is to promote civil discourse and communities of learners. Honesty sometimes hurts, and if we expect our students (or our faculty and staff) to deal with their prejudices and biases, there will be some hurt, some pain, consequential of the hoped-for honesty. What we need to have in place to allow that discourse to remain civil and communicative is a campus community predicated upon trust and civility, the nurturance of which requires a never-ending commitment from all involved.

Anyone who has accepted seriously the challenge of building a truly diverse learning community on his or her campus must become familiar with many of the items in the bibliography attached to this chapter. Too often, we in academia spend extraordinary time and energy reinventing wheels and then spinning them endlessly. So many good models exist already (whether one is talking about recruitment, bridge programs, learning communities, retention, or pedagogical strategies which benefit students of all color and nature, faculty and staff development, and anything else pertaining to our concern with "diversity" and "cultural pluralism" on campus) that we need to take the time to read about what already has been attempted, studied, measured, and proven successful in certain campus environments. Beginning with Astin, Boyer, Chickering, and Cross, and moving to Tinto and others, one can find all of the ideas, inspiration, guidelines, and programmatic formats one needs. We must know the options and then use creative imagination to accommodate and adapt ideas to fit a particular campus culture, make the commitment, take the risk, and move forward.

Notes

1. Yates, Albert C. "Parting Thoughts," *Colorado State University Alumni Magazine* (Winter 1995–96): 48.
2. Ibid.
3. Marable, Manning. *The Crisis of Color and Democracy: Essays on Race, Class, and Power.* Monroe, Maine: Common Courage Press, 1992.
4. Williams, Patricia. *The Alchemy of Race and Rights.* Cambridge: Harvard Univerity Press, 1991.
5. West, Cornel. *Race Matters.* New York: Vintage Books, 1994.
6. Lauter, Paul "'Political Correctness' and the Attack on American Colleges," in *Higher Education Under Fire: Politics, Economics, and the Crisis of the Humanities,* edited by Michael Berube and Cary Nelson. New York: Routledge, 1995.
7. Boyer, Ernest. *College: The Undergraduate Experience in America.* New York: Harper & Row, 1987.
8. Boyer, Ernest. *Campus Life: In Search of Community.* Princeton: Carnegie Foundation for the Advancement of Teaching, 1990.
9. Ibid.

[10]Richardson, Richard C., Jr. and Alfredo G. de los Santos, Jr. "Ten Principles for Good Institutional Practice in Removing Race/Ethnicity as a Factor in College Completion." In *A Crucial Agenda: Making Colleges and Universities Work Better for Minority Students*, eds. Morgan Odell and Jere J. Mock. Boulder, CO:WICHE, 1989, pp. 71–77.

[11]American Council on Education. *Educating One-Third of a Nation*. Washington, DC: ACE, 1988; Atwell, Robert H. "Minority Participation in Higher Education: We Need a New Momentum." ACE Annual Meeting Remarks. Washington, DC: ACE, 1988; Epps, Edgar G., ed. *Cultural Pluralism*. Berkeley: McCutchan Publishing, 1974; Kerschner, Lee. *Quality and Equity: The Continuing Dialogue*. Washington, DC: AASCU, 1990; Kolodny, Annette. "Colleges Must Recognize Students' Cognitive Styles and Cultural Backgrounds," *Chronicle of Higher Education*, (Feb. 6, 1991): A44; and Kozol, Jonathan. *Savage Inequalities: Children In America's Schools*. New York: Crown Publishers, 1991.

[12]American Association of State Colleges and Universities. *To Secure the Blessings of Liberty: Report of the National Commission on the Role and Future of State Colleges and Universities*. Washington, DC: AASCU, 1986, p. 9

[13]Astin, Alexander W., *Assessment for Excellence: The Philosophy and Practice of Assessment and Evaluation in Higher Education*. New York: Macmillan Publishing Company, 1991, pp. 198, 212.

[14]Payne, N. Joyce. "Hidden Messages in the Pursuit of Equality, *Academe*, 75 (Sept.–Oct. 1989):21.

[15]Richardson, Richard Jr., and Elizabeth F. Skinner. *Achieving Quality and Diversity: Universities in a Multicultural Society*. New York: Macmillan Publishing Company, Inc., 1991, pp. 22–3.

[16]Ibid., p. 4.

[17]Boyer, Ernest. *Campus Life*, op. cit.

[18]Hooks, Bell. *Teaching to Transgress: Education as the Practice of Freedom*. New York: Rontledge, 1994.

[19]Ibid.

[20]Ibid.

[21]Ibid.

[22]Jones, Joel M. "The Art of Teaching: An Act of Love." In Jean Civikly (ed.), *Communicating in College Classrooms*. San Francisco: Jossey-Bass, 1986.

Bibliography

American Association of Colleges and Universities. *American Pluralism and the College Curriculum: Higher Education in a Diverse Democracy.* Report of American Commitments Initiative of AACU. Washington, DC: AACU, 1995.

American Association of Colleges and Universities. *The Drama of Diversity and Democracy: Higher Education and American Commitments.* Report of American Commitments Initiative of AACU. Washington, DC: AACU, 1995.

American Association of State Colleges and Universities. *Minorities in Public Higher Education: At a Turning Point.* Washington, DC: AASCU, 1988.

American Association of State Colleges and Universities. *To Secure the Blessings of Liberty: Report of the National Commission on the Role and Future of State Colleges and Universities.* Washington, DC: AASCU, 1986.

American Council on Education. *Educating One-Third of a Nation.* Washington, DC: ACE, 1988.

American Council on Education. *Making the Case for Affirmative Action in Higher Education.* Washington, DC: ACE, 1996.

Anaya, Rudolfo A. *Bless Me Ultima.* Berkeley: Quinto Sol Publishers, 1972.

Appel, Morgan, et al. *The Impact of Diversity on Students: A Preliminary Review of the Research Literature.* Washington, DC: AACU, 1996.

Association of American Colleges. *Integrity in the College Curriculum: A Report to the Academic Community.* Washington, DC: AAC, 1985.

Astin, Alexander W. *Achieving Educational Excellence.* San Francisco: Jossey-Bass, 1985.

Astin, Alexander W. *Assessment for Excellence: The Philosophy and Practice of Assessment and Evaluation in Higher Education.* New York: Macmillan Publishing Company, 1991.

Atwell, Robert H. "Opening the American Mind: Fairness, Consensus, and the Role of the Academy." ACE Annual Meeting Remarks. Washington, DC: ACE, 1991.

Atwell, Robert H. "Minority Participation in Higher Education: We Need a New Momentum." ACE Annual Meeting Remarks. Washington, DC: ACE, 1988.

Banks, James A. *Teaching Strategies for Ethnic Studies.* Fifth ed. Needham Heights, MA: Allyn and Bacon, Inc., 1991.

Barber, Benjamin. *An Aristocracy of Everyone: The Politics of Education and the Future of America.* New York: Ballantine Books, 1992.

Benally, Suzanne, Jere J. Mock, and Morgan Odell (Eds.). *Pathways to the Multicultural Community: Leadership, Belonging, and Involvement.* Boulder, Colorado: WICHE, 1996.

Berry, Thomas. "The American College in the Ecological Age," in *The Dream of the Earth*. San Francisco: Sierra Club, 1988.

Birkerts, Sven. *The Gutenberg Elegies: The Fate of Reading in an Electronic Age*. New York: Fawcett Columbine, 1994.

Birnbaum, Robert. "Administrative Commitments and Minority Enrollments: College Presidents' Goals for Quality and Access," *The Review of Higher Education*, 11 (Summer, '88): 435–57.

Bowser, Benjamin P. *Confronting Diversity Issues on Campus*. Newbury Park, CA: Sage Publications, 1993.

Boyer, Ernest L. *Campus Life: In Search of Community*. Princeton: Carnegie Foundation for the Advancement of Teaching, 1990.

Boyer, Ernest L. *College: The Undergraduate Experience in America*. New York: Harper & Row, 1987.

Boyer, Ernest L. "Reflections on the Great Debate," in *Excellence in Education*, edited by Philip Altbach and Associates. Buffalo: Prometheus Books, 1985, pp. 43–55.

Boyer, Ernest L. *Scholarship Reconsidered: Priorities of the Professoriate*. Princeton: Carnegie Foundation for the Advancement of Teaching, 1990.

Bruner, Jerome S. "Toward a Sense of Community," in James Bowman, et al., *Of Education and Human Community*. Lincoln, Nebraska: University of Nebraska Press, 1972, pp. 77–81.

Carnegie Commission for Higher Education. *Quality and Equality: Levels of Federal Responsibility for Higher Education*. New York: McGraw-Hill, 1968.

Carter, David, and Alice Chandler. "Fostering a Multi-Cultural Curriculum: Principles for Presidents." *AASCU Issues* (1990).

Carter, Deborah J., and Reginald Wilson. *Fourteenth Annual Status Report on Minorities in Higher Education*. Washington, DC: ACE, 1996.

Chickering, Arthur W. and Associates. *The Modern American College: Responding to the New Realities of Diverse Students and a Changing Society*. San Francisco: Jossey-Bass, 1981.

Chickering, Arthur W., and Zelda Gamson. "Seven Principles for Good Practice in Undergraduate Education." *AAHE Bulletin*, 1987 (Vol. 39): 3–7.

Coles, Robert. *The Call of Stories: Teaching and the Moral Imagination*. Boston: Houghton Mifflin, 1989.

Coles, Robert. "Hispanic Dreams/American Dreams: In Search of a New Heritage," *Change*, 20 (May–June 1988): 12–13.

The College Board. "Educational Access and Achievement in America," in *Proceedings of the Twentieth Anniversary of the Washington Office*. New York: College Entrance Examination Board, 1987.

Cortes, Carlos. "Pluribus & Unum: The Quest for Community Amid Diversity," *Change*, 23 (September–October 1991): 8–13.

Craige, Betty Jean. *Laying the Ladder Down: The Emergence of Cultural Holism*. Amherst, MA: University of Massachusetts Press, 1992.

Daniels, Lee A. "Diversity, Correctness, & Campus Life," *Change*, 23 (September–October 1991): 16–20.

Duster, Troy. "Understanding Self-Segregation on the Campus," *Chronicle of Higher Education*, (Sept. 25, 1991): B1–2.

Dye, Nancy. "What Color Is Your Reading List?" *New York Times Book Review*, (March 31, 1991): 12.

Emerson, Ralph Waldo. "The American Scholar." First published 1837, reprinted in *The American Scholar Today*, edited by David Mead. New York: Dodd, Mean, and Co., 1970.

Etzioni, Amatai. *The Spirit of Community*. New York: Crown Publishers, Inc., 1993.

Epps, Edgar G., ed. *Cultural Pluralism*. Berkeley: McCutchan Publishing, 1974.

Estrada, Leonardo F. "Anticipating the Demographic Future: Dramatic Changes are on the Way," *Change*, 20 (May–June 1988): 14–19.

Farney, Dennis. "Mosaic of Hope: Ethnic Identities Clash with Student Idealism at a California College," *The Wall Street Journal* (Dec. 2, 1992): A–1, A–6.

Fedullo, Mick. *Light of the Feather: A Teacher's Journey into Native American Classrooms and Culture*. New York: Doubleday, 1992.

Gabelnick, Faith, J. MacGregor, R.S. Matthews, and B.L. Smith. *Learning Communities: Creating Connections among Students, Faculty, and Disciplines*. San Francisco: Jossey-Bass, 1990.

Gainen, Joanne, and Robert Boice (Eds.). *Building a Diverse Faculty*. San Francisco: Jossey-Bass, 1993.

Gamson, Zelda F., and Associates. *Liberating Education*. San Francisco: Jossey-Bass, 1990.

Gardner, Howard. *Multiple Intelligences: The Theory in Practice*. New York: Basic Books, 1993.

Gardner, John. *Excellence: Can We Be Equal and Excellent Too?* New York: W.W. Norton, 1987 (new ed.).

Gates, Henry Louis, Jr. *Loose Canons*. New York: Oxford University Press, 1993.

Giamatti, A. Bartlett. *A Free and Ordered Space: The Real World of the University*. New York: W.W. Norton & Co., 1988.

Gittell, Marilyn and Bruce Dohler. "Cultural Pluralism: Traditional and Alternative Models in Higher Education." in *Badges and Indicia of Slavery: Cultural Pluralism Redefined*, edited by Antonia Pantoja, Barbara Blourock and James Bowman. Lincoln, Nebraska: University of Nebraska Press, 1975, pp. 26–123.

Goleman, Daniel. *Emotional Intelligence*. New York: Bantam Books, 1995.

Gordon, Avery F., and Christopher Newfield (Eds). *Mapping Multiculturalism*. Minneapolis: University of Minnesota Press, 1996.

Graff, Gerald. *Beyond the Culture Wars: How Teaching the Conflicts Can Revitalize American Education*. New York: W. W. Norton and Co., 1992.

Grant, Carl A., and Christine E. Sleeter, "Equality, Equity, and Excellence: A Critique," in *Excellence in Education: Perspectives on Policy and Practice*, edited by Philip Altbach and Associates. Buffalo: Prometheus Books, 1985, pp. 139–160.

Green, Madeleine (Ed.). *Minorities on Campus: A Handbook for Enhancing Diversity*. Washington, DC: ACE, 1990.

Greene, Maxine. *Landscapes of Learning*. New York: Teachers College Press, 1978.

Halberstam, David. *The Next Century*. New York: William Morrow & Co., 1991.

Halcon, John J. "Exemplary Programs for College-Bound Minority Students," in *A Crucial Agenda: Making Colleges and Universities Work Better for Minority Students*, edited by Morgan Odell and Jere J. Mock. Boulder, Colorado: WICHE, 1989, pp. 79–117.

Hansen, W. Lee, and Jacob Stampen. "Economics and Financing of Higher Education: The Tension Between Quality and Equality," in Philip Altbach and Robert Bendahl (Eds.). *Higher Education in American Society*. Buffalo: Prometheus Books, 1981, pp. 107–128.

Hively, Robert (ed.). *The Lurking Evil: Racial and Ethnic Conflict on the College Campus*. Washington, DC: AASCU, 1990.

Hooks, Bell. *Teaching to Transgress: Education as the Practice of Freedom*. New York: Routledge, 1994.

Hurtado, Sylvia. "The Campus Racial Climate: Contexts for Conflict." *Journal of Higher Education* 63 (5), 1992: 539–69.

Jacoby, Russell. *Dogmatic Wisdom: How the Culture Wars Divert Education and Distract America*. New York: Doubleday, 1994.

Jones, Joel M. "The Art of Teaching: An Act of Love." In Jean Civikly (ed.), *Communicating in College Classrooms*. San Francisco: Jossey-Bass, 1986.

Jones, Joel M. "The Liberal Art of Community Building: From Aristotle to Anaya, Socrates to Silko," in *Pathways to the Multicultural Community: Leadership, Belonging, and Involvement*, edited by Benally, Suzanne, Jere J. Mock, and Morgan Odell. Boulder, Colorado: WICHE, 1996.

Kerschner, Lee. *Quality and Equity: The Continuing Dialogue*. Washington, DC: AASCU, 1990.

Kolodny, Annette. "Colleges Must Recognize Students' Cognitive Styles and Cultural Backgrounds," *Chronicle of Higher Education*, (Feb. 6, 1991): A44.

Kozol, Jonathan. *Savage Inequalities: Children In America's Schools*. New York: Crown Publishers, 1991.

Kuh, George D., J. H. Schuh, E. J. Whitt, and Assoc. *Involving Colleges: Successful Approaches to Fostering Student Learning and Development Outside the Classroom*. San Francisco: Jossey-Bass, 1991.

Lauter, Paul. "'Political Correctness' and the Attack on American Colleges," in *Higher Education Under Fire: Politics, Economics, and the Crisis of the Humanities*, edited by Michael Berube and Cary Nelson. New York: Routledge, 1995.

Levine, Arthur. "The Meaning of Diversity," *Change*, 23 (September–October 1991): 4–5.

Levine, Arthur, and Associates. *Shaping Higher Education's Future: Demographic Realities and Opportunities, 1990–2000*. San Francisco: Jossey-Bass, 1989.

Marable, Manning. *The Crisis of Color and Democracy: Essays on Race, Class and Power*. Monroe, Maine: Common Courage Press, 1992.

Mayhew, Louis B., and Associates. *The Quest for Quality: The Challenge for Undergraduate Education in the 1990s*. San Francisco: Jossey-Bass, 1990.

McDermott, John J. *Streams of Experience: Reflections on the History and Philosophy of American Culture*. Amherst, Massachusetts: University of Massachusetts Press, 1986.

McGee, Leo. "What Makes a Predominantly White Campus an 'Inviting Campus' for Black Students?" *Black Issues in Higher Education* 7 (13), 1990: 72.

Mingle, James R., and Esther Rodriguez (Eds.). *Building Coalitions for Minority Success*. Denver: State Higher Education Executive Officers, 1990.

Minnich, Elizabeth K. "Liberal Arts and Civic Arts: Education for `The Free Man'?" *Liberal Education*, (Winter 1982): 311–21.

Minnich, Elizabeth K. *Liberal Learning and the Arts of Connection for the New Academy*. Washington, DC: AACU, 1995.

National Center for Higher Education Management Systems. *Planning, Managing, and Financing in the 1980's: Achieving Excellence, Diversity, and Access in the Context of*

Stable Resources and Demands for Increased Productivity. Boulder, Colorado: NCHEMS, 1978.

National Task Force for Minority Achievement in Higher Education. *Achieving Campus Diversity: Policies for Change.* Denver: Education Commission of the States, 1990.

Newman, Frank. *Choosing Quality: Reducing Conflict Between the State and the University.* Denver: Education Commission of the States, 1987.

Odell, Morgan, and Jere J. Mock (Eds.). *A Crucial Agenda: Making Colleges and Universities Work Better for Minority Students.* Boulder, Colorado: WICHE, 1989.

Palmer, Parker. *To Know as We Are Known: A Spirituality of Education.* San Francisco: Harper and Row, 1983.

Pascarella, Ernest T., et al., "Influences on Students' Openness to Diversity and Challenge in the First Year of College." *The Journal of Higher Education* (March/April 1996), Vol. 67: 174–195.

Pascarella, Ernest T., and Patrick T. Terenzini. *How College Affects Students.* San Francisco: Jossey-Bass, 1991.

Payne, N. Joyce. "Hidden Messages in the Pursuit of Equality," *Academe,* 75 (September–October 1989): pp. 19–22.

Quality Education for Minorities Project. *Education That Works: An Action Plan for the Education of Minorities.* Cambridge, Massachusetts: MIT, 1990.

Richardson, Richard C., Jr. *Promoting Fair College Outcomes: Learning from the Experiences of the Past Decade.* Denver: Education Commission of the States, 1991.

Richardson, Richard C., Jr. and L.W. Bender. *Fostering Minority Access and Achievement in Higher Education.* San Francisco: Jossey-Bass, 1987.

Richardson, Richard C., Jr. and Alfredo G. de los Santos, Jr. (Eds.). *From Access to Achievement: Fulfilling the Promise.* Special edition of *The Review of Higher Education,* 11 (Summer 1988).

Richardson, Richard C., Jr. and Alfredo G. de los Santos, Jr. "Ten Principles for Good Institutional Practice in Removing Race/Ethnicity as a Factor in College Completion." In *A Crucial Agenda: Making Colleges and Universities Work Better for Minority Students,* eds. Morgan Odell and Jere J. Mock. Boulder, CO:WICHE, 1989, pp. 71–77.

Richardson, Richard C., Jr. and Elizabeth F. Skinner. *Achieving Quality and Diversity: Universities in a Multicultural Society.* New York: Macmillan Publishing Co., 1991.

Roberts, Helen, et al. *Teaching from a Multicultural Perspective.* Thousand Oaks, CA: Sage Publications, 1994.

Rudolph, Frederick. *Curriculum: A History of the American Undergraduate Course of Study Since 1636.* San Francisco: Jossey-Bass, 1977.

Sandler, Bernice R., et al. *The Chilly Classroom Climate: A Guide to Improve the Education of Women.* Washington, DC: The National Association for Women in Education, 1996.

Saufley, Ronald W., Kathryn O. Cowan, and J. Herman Blake. "The Struggles of Minority Students at Predominantly White Institutions," in *Teaching Minority Students.* J. H. Cones, III, J.F. Noonan, D. Janha, eds. New Directions for Teaching and Learning, No. 16. San Francisco: Jossey-Bass, December 1983.

Schaefer, William D. *Education Without Compromise: From Chaos to Coherence in Higher Education.* San Francisco: Jossey-Bass, 1990.

Schlesinger, Arthur M., Jr. *The Disuniting of America: Reflections on a Multicultural Society.* Knoxville, Tennessee: Whittle Books, 1991.

Schmitz, Betty. *Core Curriculum and Cultural Pluralism: A Guide for Campus Planners.* Washington, DC: AAC, 1992.

Schoem, David, et al. (Eds). *Multicultural Teaching in the University.* West Port, Conneticut: Praeger, 1993.

Seneca, Joseph J., and Michael K. Taussig. "Educational Quality, Access, and Tuition Policy at State Universities," *The Journal of Higher Education,* 58 (January–February 1987): 25–37.

Silko, Leslie Marmon. *Ceremony.* New York: The Viking Press, 1977.

Smith, Daryl G. *The Challenge of Diversity: Involvement or Alienation in the Academy?* Report No. 5, ASHE-ERIC Monograph Series. Washington DC: School of Education and Human Development, George Washington University, 1989.

Smith, Duane A. *Sacred Trust: The Birth and Development of Fort Lewis College.* Boulder: University Press of Colorado, 1991.

Smith, Page. *Killing the Spirit: Higher Education in America.* New York: Viking, 1990.

Smith, Virginia, and Alison Bernstein. *The Impersonal Campus.* San Francisco: Jossey-Bass, 1979.

Steiner, George. *Language and Silence: Essays on Language, Literature, and the Inhuman.* New York: Atheneum, 1967.

Taggart, Leslie, (Ed.). *Emerging Voices: A Cross-Cultural Reader.* Fort Worth, Texas: Holt Rinehart and Winston, Inc., 1990.

Taylor, Harold. *Students Without Teachers: The Crisis in the University.* New York: McGraw-Hill, 1969.

Tinto, Vincent. *Leaving College: Rethinking the Causes and Cures of Student Attrition.* Chicago: The University of Chicago Press, 1993.

Toffler, Alvin. *Power Shift: Knowledge, Wealth and Violence at the Edge of the 21st Century.* New York: Bantam Books, 1990.

Vendler, Helen. "MLA Presidential Address 1980," in Robert Bellah and Associates. *Individualism and Commitment in American Life*. New York: Harper & Row, 1987.

Warch, Richard. "Communities of Mind and Spirit." *Liberal Education*, 1990 (Vol. 76): 7–13.

Weis, Lois. "Excellence and Student Class, Race, and Gender Cultures," in Philip Altbach, et al. (Eds.). *Excellence in Education: Perspectives on Policy and Practice*. Buffalo: Prometheus Books, 1985, pp. 217–232.

West, Cornel. *Race Matters*. New York: Vintage Books, 1994.

Western Interstate Commission for Higher Education. *The Road to College: Educational Progress by Race and Ethnicity*. Boulder, Colorado: WICHE, 1991.

Williams, Patricia J. *The Alchemy of Race and Rights*. Cambridge: Harvard University Press, 1991.

Wilshire, Bruce. *The Moral Collapse of the University: Professionalism, Purity, and Alienation*. Albany, New York: State University of New York Press, 1990.

Wilson, Reginald, and Deborah Carter. *14th Annual Status Report on Minorities in Higher Education*. Washington, DC:ACE, 1996.

Wong, Frank F. "Diversity and Our Discontents," *AAHE Bulletin* 45 (2), 1992: 3–5.

Yates, Albert C. "Parting Thoughts" *Colorado State University Alumni Magazine* (Winter 1995–96): 48.

Improving Student Retention: The Role of the University President

Ruben Armiñana
President
Sonoma State University

Drew Calandrella
Associate Vice President
Student Academic Services
Sonoma State University

Donald Farish
Provost and Vice President
for Academic Affairs
Sonoma State University

Introduction

The role of the public university president has never been more important than it is in today's higher education environment of budget constraints, increased public scrutiny, legislative intrusion, student demands, and competition from private universities and the newly emerging nontraditional purveyors of higher education. With the reality of decreased budgetary support from the state, an increasing interest from legislators and citizens in general regarding the productivity and efficiency of public institutions, and a gnawing realization that the current ways of operating universities will not be able to meet the needs of the "tidal wave" of college-age students expected to hit the campuses by the turn of the century, universities are being forced to rethink how students will be recruited, advised, instructed, and graduated.

It is already the case that the number of traditional-age students is increasing at many public universities. This is certainly the case for Sonoma State University, where both the absolute number and the percentage of freshmen have been growing each year. With significant increases in tuition and fees at public universities (including Sonoma), students and taxpayers alike are asking hard questions about the outcome of their investment in public higher education.

Recent articles in the media have focused on the need for students to graduate in a timely fashion, as the tax dollars that subsidize their education are being viewed as a limited resource—especially given the number of students looking to higher education as the way to a secure future given the perception that the baccalaureate is a necessity for success in the job market and the community. Some of these articles propose that students with excessive units—more units earned than necessary for a baccalaureate—be denied the public subsidy and pay the full cost of their courses.

While any one of these environmental factors might be expected to occupy considerable time and energy, the college or university president is the individual to whom the faculty, state system, legislature (or governor), students, and community look to provide leadership. Often, due to the critical nature of particular situations, the problems facing university presidents do not allow the type of consultation which most campuses have come to expect. For example, many of the problems on campuses involving budget or other resource allocation situations require a prompt response, and the president often is placed in the unenviable position of having to make tough decisions that are then promptly criticized.

Other problems may appear at first glance not to share the immediacy of a budget crisis, but they ultimately may lead to budget problems if allowed to continue unresolved. One such problem facing most public university presidents is the retention and graduation of students. While many believe that the issue of retaining students is a campus-wide or system-wide problem, student attrition is not even on the radar of many campus community members. Yet according to Vincent Tinto, "More students leave their college or university prior to degree completion than stay. . . . The consequences of this massive and continuing exodus from higher education are not trivial, either for the individuals who leave or for their institutions."

With the economic stakes for college students so high, their success in college is certainly an important individual goal. The gap in annual wages between those with a college degree and those with a high school diploma increases each year. College graduates earn nearly twice what high school graduates do, and their unemployment rate is significantly lower (3.5 percent) than that (8 percent) of high school grads. Moreover, while a college degree is not the only road successful and meaningful life, it certainly is true that a college degree can open occupational or professional doors that are closed to those without a degree.

> In round numbers, a college diploma earns an annual return—after accounting for inflation—of 13 to 14 percent on its costs. That beats the long-run returns on stocks. It swamps the returns on bonds. It explains why your daughter or son wouldn't be better off if she or he invested the money and went to work immediately after high school. Kevin Murphy, an economics professor at the University of Chicago, found that in 1980 a college worker earned about 43 percent more an hour than a worker with only a high school diploma. By 1994 that earnings advantage had ballooned to 73 percent. "The premium attached to a college degree may be as high as 75 to 80 percent now," says Murphy. . . .

> Even at the most primitive level—employment—people who hold a college degree are better off. Rates of unemployment are three times higher for 25- to 29-year-olds with only a high school diploma than for those with a college education.

> —*Forbes*, November 18, 1995

Monthly Earnings by Level of Education, 1990

Four-Year College Degree	$2,100
Community College Degree	$1,700
High School Diploma	$1,100
Non-High School Diploma	$500

Source: Southern Regional Education Board

For admissions offices at universities, retention problems present challenges. In addition to recruiting each new entering class, admissions offices need to replace students who leave. Also, because most public universities rely on some form of headcount or full-time equivalency as the basis of their state allocations, high levels of student attrition can have a direct impact on a campus's base budget. With the average graduation rates of public universities barely exceeding 50 percent, the various legislatures and their constituencies are more than a little interested in how efficiently scarce state dollars are being used. Not many businesses would succeed if only half their "products" successfully completed their process and made it to market.

However, student attrition historically has been not only tolerated but openly accepted as a necessary consequence of maintaining quality. To be sure, students leave for many reasons, only some of which can be influenced by the university. Such variables as size of student body (campus is too large/small), distance from home (campus is too far/close), severe familial financial crises (loss of jobs), social pressures (loneliness, love relationships), family member or student health problems (including abuse of alcohol and drugs) are just some examples of factors over which campuses have no control. Students leaving for the above reasons ultimately may complete their degrees, though they may not return to the same institution to do so.

However, there are several dimensions of the student experience over which an institution does have control, and collectively, these contribute to students' overall satisfaction with their college experience and their retention and graduation rates. Examples include students' identification with the college—its environment, culture, and sense of community; students' feeling connected to a larger community on the campus; a challenging and stimulating academic and intellectual environment; students' belief that the campus is supportive of their academic progress and needs; and the experience of connecting with at least one faculty or professional employee who pays attention to their development. Many other examples could be given, but our point is to highlight some of the less tangible student experiences in the higher education enterprise—experiences which often are overlooked.

Each fall term, campuses across the country welcome new students, help them move into residence halls, direct them to the bookstore, and arm them with campus maps so they can find the buildings in which their classes meet. How receptive an individual campus is to new students determines the very important and lasting impressions the students form.

Culture Shock

Dorothy's statement in *The Wizard of Oz* that "We're not in Kansas anymore" highlights students' initial experiences on campus. For many it can only be described as culture shock.

Most of us have experienced some amount of culture shock at some point in our lives. Anyone who has moved to a new country, state, city, or employer has had to deal with the necessary adjustment to the new "culture"—its mores, values, traditions, language, foods, services, to name just a few aspects thereof. If we succeeded in the transition, then we continued and, hopefully, prospered in that environment; in higher education, that is the idea of retention. Failure to integrate into the culture usually results in one leaving that culture—"attrition" in higher education terms.

Boyer, in his study of American higher education in 1987, concluded that "new students have little sense of being inducted into a community whose structure, privileges, and responsibilities have been evolving for almost a millennium." Students who leave the culture of their homes and high schools or community colleges and adjust to the culture of the university undergo culture shock.

Each campus must ask: What is the role of faculty and staff in helping new students assimilate into the campus culture?

Each fall semester, Sonoma State University welcomes approximately 850 first-time freshmen with their varied cultures. (The strategies discussed here focus on freshmen, but we are concerned with the retention of all students. Until graduation, all students are considered "at risk.") All of these freshmen have left their cultures of high school and family and community, along with their structures and mores. Assimilation is neither easy nor automatic; for many, the experience of being away from home for the first time is both exciting and overwhelming. Yet the assimilation process has a significant impact on the entire SSU community. New students do not appear to speak our language, they often do not share the same interests as the faculty, and at times, they do not appear to take their studies seriously.

Assimilation into a culture is not a trivial feat, but it is largely invisible. This is because the ability to cope with change is largely an individual process that different people work out in different ways.

To the extent that the experience of students entering the university can be understood, strategies to improve their retention, satisfaction, and graduation can be developed and implemented. Since the above discussion spoke to the experience of the individual student as she enters the culture of the university, the campus response to all students' experience is even more potent in terms of helping to enhance their retention.

Retention programs abound on campuses and range from "freshman year experience" courses to selected advising programs for "at risk" students, as well as other variations. If these programs exist as interventions without direct connection to the academic enterprise and are not valued by the campus in terms of their contribution to students' development, then their effects on student retention will be limited.

Conversely, if student retention, graduation, and satisfaction are made a key institutional priority—for example, the president expresses this priority almost daily to all groups he meets, from prospective students and their parents to new faculty, donors, and public officials—and if programs are developed with the appropriate academic connections, coupled with recognition for those campus members participating in the programs, then retention and graduation can be positively influenced. That is, leadership from the top—especially from the campus president—is essential for increasing student retention, satisfaction, and graduation. Such leadership helps bring retention into the ethos, and ultimately, into the culture, of the campus.

What follows is a recounting of events as they unfolded at Sonoma State University. At the faculty convocation in January 1993, President Armiñana challenged the campus community by requesting that the provost initiate a number of studies of issues pertinent to shepherding Sonoma into the 21st century. The provost organized the challenge by calling for participation and by appointing a series of task forces comprising of faculty members and staff.

Principal among the issues for study was improving the retention, satisfaction, and graduation of Sonoma students. Retaining and graduating students was just as important as recruiting and enrolling them.

A task force met during the fall 1993 semester and provided the provost with the following recommendations:

- Appoint a Retention and Graduation Steering Committee charged with designing retention/graduation programs for the university and improving retention programs and services for SSU students.

- Support the enrollment management efforts of admissions and records and such new initiatives as the "Enrollment Confirmation Deposit" and the New Student Scholarship program ($1,000 scholarships to those admitted and confirmed freshmen with a 4.0 GPA).

- Support the initiatives of institutional research (IR) in collecting information from the Astin Freshman Survey, focus groups, development of exit interview processes, and longitudinal studies which would provide comparative data for use by SSU.

- Organize all of the student services in the university as a Retention Services Division or organize academically related services as a unit within Academic Affairs. That is, develop an integrated and comprehensive set of retention services, along with student life services, in order to make advising meaningful and productive for students.

- Develop a "customer service" approach to working with students that is embraced by every staff and faculty member of the campus community so that student satisfaction is increased. Create a campus environment that supports students' academic and social development through orientation, transitional issues, and out of classroom time.

During the January 1994 faculty convocation, President Armiñana acknowledged the response to his challenge and introduced the concept of the "Educational Mentoring Team" (EMT). During a faculty retreat that spring, he described the EMT as a means by which students would have a "structured relationship with a stable and identifiable group of academic and student services professionals who know them personally and care for them."

The provost circulated a draft of his position paper, "Improving Retention, Graduation, and Student Satisfaction at Sonoma State University," at a department chairs breakfast on March 27, 1994. The paper had been written to inform the campus about retention at SSU and proposed the Educational Mentoring Team concept as a framework for beginning to address complex retention and graduation issues. Input was solicited during this meeting and at subsequent meetings throughout the campus.

Subsequent to the beginning of the Educational Mentoring Team program, the university was engaged in several organizational changes which resulted in the formation of the Student Academic Services unit in the Academic Affairs Division. This return of student services essential to the academic program signalled recognition of the important role of such programs as residential life, financial aid, academic advising, career services, international student programs, the educational opportunity program, the tutorial program, learning skills, and the orientation program in attracting, retaining, and graduating students. More important, all of the members of the EMT were not in the same division; thus, many of the problems that typically arise when faculty and staff from different divisions are expected to work together were avoided. This new unit was led by the former associate dean of student affairs, who was given the new title of associate vice president (of academic affairs) for student academic services.

The final step was formulation of a work plan to operationalize SSU's Educational Mentoring Team Program. Calls for participation to both faculty and student affairs professionals yielded the first eight teams; these served as the pioneering Educational Mentoring Teams during fall 1994. A steering committee was formed to further refine and organize the program.

SSU Educational Mentoring Team Program Description

The charge to the Educational Mentoring Team Program is to contribute to the retention of students at Sonoma State University through the coordination, facilitation, and delivery of essential services to matriculating students from the point of entry into the university through graduation.

Each EMT consists of one student affairs professional, one faculty member, and a peer mentor who works in partnership to provide retention services to a cohort of freshman students. During the first year of the program (1994–95), the cohort included 80 students (only 12 EMTs were in place). Each of the past two years has had cohorts of approximately 40 students for each EMT. In 1997–98, the cohort will be further reduced to 25, and each will be linked to a section of a freshman GE class.

Each entering freshman is assigned to an EMT during summer orientation, which is attended by approximately 90 percent of all incoming freshmen. EMT members provide all of the freshman advising during the orientation programs. The freshmen are also encouraged to enroll in a section of a two-unit freshman seminar (University 102) taught by the faculty and staff of each EMT; by so doing, students benefit from continued contact with their EMT throughout their first semester at the university.

The seminar covers such topics as:
- the meaning, value, and expectations of a college education;
- making the transition to college from high school;
- problem solving and decision making;
- selecting a college major and a future career;
- goal setting and motivation;
- navigating the university curriculum—how to graduate in four years;
- learning how to learn—study skills and success in college;
- managing time and stress; and
- interpersonal relations and related student life-style responsibilities regarding wellness, alcohol and drug use, sexual harassment, and many other topics.

Over the three years of the EMT program, some 80 percent of entering freshmen have initially enrolled in the course; census registration indicates that approximately 70 percent have actually enrolled.

When the freshman-assured computer access program was implemented in 1995, the freshman seminar proved an invaluable source for orienting students to the many networked information resources available on campus.

Each EMT consults with other campus team members to solve problems and to help students obtain technical assistance as appropriate. Such team members include the appropriate admissions and records staff, financial aid representative, residence life staff, Educational Opportunity Program (EOP) staff, and so on.

The EMT maintains contact with students through formal (instruction, mid-semester evaluation) and informal (social) activities. The EMT also makes referrals to such student services as counseling, the Women's Resource Center, reentry, and international student programs, as appropriate, for help with particular needs or interests. This advising relationship continues beyond the freshman year until the students are "handed off" to their major departments for academic advisement. The EMT members remain accessible to assigned students for ongoing advising and assistance through graduation from SSU. This ensures that each SSU student has at least two faculty/staff members to help guide him through his academic career at SSU and to help enhance his satisfaction with his experience at the university.

Students frequently return to their EMT during their sophomore and junior years to check in with advisors and follow up on concerns they may have regarding their academic progress (or other issues they may encounter while attending the university). Although the number of students participating beyond their freshman year is not overwhelming, a steady stream of students does maintain contact with the various EMT members, particularly during the advising time of the semester.

EMT Outcomes

The outcomes to date, as reported by the Institutional Research Office, reveal that since the first year of EMT, the percentage of freshmen returning from fall to spring has increased steadily from 87 percent to 93 percent, and the percentage of freshmen returning as sophomores has increased as well.

The freshman class continues to carry the highest average unit load each term, and this is a direct reflection of the advising they are receiving through summer orientation and their first term.

With a mid-semester evaluation taking place each term, first-time freshmen are beginning to access learning assistance programs more frequently; there is even an indication that fewer freshmen are finding themselves on academic probation. In fact, grade point averages are improving.

While the Educational Mentoring Teams are not the sole source of improvements in retention, they have helped foster a campuswide commitment to improving retention and graduation rates. For this reason, Sonoma State University is one of eight campuses nationwide participating in the AASCU/Sallie Mae Retention survey that has reported steady improvement in six-year graduation rates over the four years of the survey's administration.

The Role of the President

The single most important leverage point within the university to bring about change is commitment from the leadership. The Sonoma campus has three goals: increased retention, graduation, and student satisfaction. These are the goals of the president, and they are articulated often and in a variety of public and private venues.

Reinforcing this commitment by way of recognition and reward is paramount to the campus's sustained support for the changes. Promotion decisions and performance-based salary increases which include consideration of participation in the Educational Mentoring Team program reinforce the importance of retention-related work on the campus.

Another point of leverage is using feedback from EMT faculty and staff to help direct policy changes. Thus, when faculty governance recommended significant changes in the advising policy, information and suggestions provided by EMT members were incorporated.

Organizational changes also serve as a point of leverage. The student affairs division was reorganized into two units: Student Academic Services was created to provide the necessary organizational support for retention services through such programs as academic advising, career services, tutoring, the Educational Opportunity Program, financial aid, residential life, the international students program, orientation, the summer bridge program, and Educational Mentoring Teams. Because this unit reports through the provost and exists on the academic side of the university, the importance of retention is reinforced directly.

Articulation of retention as a goal by the president, organizational changes, reward systems, and policy changes all contribute to recognition by the campus that retention is the responsibility of all members of the community, not just one office or division.

Advantages and Disadvantages
of Systemic Change

As with any change, especially when influenced by the president, there are advantages and disadvantages as the campus culture adjusts to the changes. Following are some examples drawn from Sonoma State's experience:

Advantages

- Systemic change affects all members of the community—students, staff, faculty, and associated external members.

- The goal of retention as a shared goal contributes to an evolving ethos of concern for students' success. This results in improved customer service from all parts of the campus community.

- Results are more dramatic because significant activity and attention are directed toward systemic change. Thus, the more intangible rewards are celebrated by those involved, and reluctant campus members begin to get involved.

- Changes in position responsibilities (such as those of student services professionals) result in more focused activities with students and reinforce the outcomes of the work being accomplished.

- New skills acquired by faculty are shared in departments (e.g., general education advising), and a synergy is created within the advising roles of faculty.

- Student learning is enhanced as it becomes the outcome of a campus engaged in student-centered retention efforts.

- New ways of working with students and other staff on campus have resulted in a greater appreciation of the roles and contributions each member brings to the campus enterprise.

- When successful and viewed as contributing to the greater good of the campus, other systemic changes are more easily accomplished. The computer access requirement was endorsed much more quickly, and, given its tie to the EMT program and an enhanced educational experience for students, the program met with little resistance.

Disadvantages

- Systemic change can be very threatening to personnel not accustomed to or comfortable with change.

- The visibility of systemic change makes the leadership more accountable for any missteps; often, such missteps are exaggerated, even as the positive aspects of the change are downplayed.

- Systemic change often equates with cultural change; as such, it is much more difficult to accomplish because it involves reexamination of campus members' long-held beliefs and assumptions about their roles and their expectations of students.

- Systemic change often requires the identification of funding. This must be accomplished without negatively impacting ongoing programs.

- Often, systemic change is held to a higher measure of accountability; declarations of success are hard-earned.

Retention and Public Accountability

Improving retention, graduation, and student satisfaction is good public policy. With California taxpayers providing the support for a subsidized (approximately 78 percent) California State University education, maximizing efforts to help students succeed helps in the following ways:

- Students receive the necessary advising and contact which aids their academic progress through difficult transitions and times of self-doubt.

- Students graduate earlier and at higher rates and become taxpayers themselves, thus helping to contribute to the very system which enabled their college education to become a reality.

- With improved retention and graduation, public universities become more efficient, and that efficiency focuses attention on their assets and contributions to society rather than on their perceived high costs.

- With the increasing cost of student attendance at public universities, public scrutiny of the value gained is increasing. Improving retention encourages the public to support the educational enterprise because it underscores the belief that the institution is contributing to an improved quality of life for the populace.

Conclusion

Through an articulated vision which was operationalized with appropriate organizational changes, recognition of the importance of the work of those involved, and continued incorporation of retention practices into the campus culture, the role of the president has been paramount in Sonoma State University's success in enhancing student retention, satisfaction, and graduation rates.

Bibliography

Boyer, E. L. College: *The Undergraduate Experience in America*. Princeton, NJ: Carnegie Foundation for the Advancement of Teaching, 1987.

Kerr, Clark. *The Uses of the University*. 3rd ed. Cambridge, MA: Harvard University Press, 1982.

Tinto, Vincent. *Leaving College: Rethinking the Causes and Cures of Student Attrition*. 2nd ed. Chicago: University of Chicago Press, 1993.

Santovec, Mary Lou (Ed.). *Building Diversity: Recruitment and Retention in the '90s*. 2nd ed. Madison, Wisconsin: Magna Publications, 1993.

A Comprehensive Approach to Enhancing Student Retention and Graduation

Vera King Farris
President
The Richard Stockton State
College of New Jersey

Higher education has become a sizable enterprise, whether measured in the number of institutions, the number of students, or the number of dollars spent on operations. However, the importance of higher education cannot be measured only by the number of students enrolled and money spent but must also be measured by the extent to which colleges and universities strengthen and enrich individuals and communities. A college education benefits both the individual and the public at large. To a remarkable degree, attending college has become an expectation of most high school graduates and their families. An equal presumption is that the student will persist until the desired academic goal has been attained, whether that goal is a degree or completion of a specific program of study.

The investment made in higher education reflects the level of confidence citizens have in its value to society. It is not surprising, therefore, that one of the most frequently used criteria to judge the performance of a college is its graduation rate.

Why Does Retention of Students Matter?

Education at the college level has become an essential element of a technologically advanced, knowledge-intensive society. Students who do not persist until graduation often cannot access the professional work environment. Given this, why are some students not able to persist?

Students' persistence toward educational goals and degree completion objectives is affected by many factors. Students who work while attending college often take fewer credits per semester. This slows their time to graduation. Some students "stop out" or "drop out" for financial or personal reasons. Yet other students need remedial courses to bridge the gap between high school courses and college subjects. Still other students have language barriers to overcome. In addition, students with educationally or economically disadvantaged backgrounds often need a longer period of study in college than students who demonstrate strong academic preparation. In some instances, the length of time to degree represents a delayed gratification which results in a student deciding to drop out of school. Although a four-year baccalaureate degree was once typical, time to complete a degree has lengthened over the past two decades. Five or six years is now the more typical time required to complete a BA or BS degree, even at colleges with good student retention records.

A Comprehensive Approach to Student Retention

Institutions that employ or embark upon a piecemeal approach to strengthening their student retention and graduation rates rarely experience long-term success for their efforts.

Sound student retention programs, like successful student recruitment programs, result from a comprehensive, all-college effort that is mission sensitive and attuned appropriately to student life both inside and outside the classroom.

Richard Stockton College of New Jersey's comprehensive approach to enhancing student retention and graduation rates has yielded measurable results. A number of the underlying programs, policies, and philosophies that have effectively supported the college's comprehensive retention effort are described in this chapter.

The Role of the Institutional Mission in Student Retention

A clear, focused mission is a key to good student retention and a strong graduation rate. The mission sets the tone for the college's priorities and provides guidance and distinction to student goal attainment. Stockton has a clearly stated mission to be a premier liberal arts and sciences college for the citizens of New Jersey. As a fairly young institution (25 years), Stockton's energies are unfettered by practices imposed by its own history. Indeed, it is the college's tradition of innovation that lies at the core of its vitality. Creative programs that enhance student retention are part of the fabric of the college.

Stockton's energy and vitality are tapped continuously as the college adjusts to a variety of external changes. What remains constant, however, is the college's strong student-oriented philosophy.

In general, the students attracted to Stockton come well prepared for college with an average total SAT score of 1131. They reflect the social, ethnic, and economic diversity of the state of New Jersey; 15 percent of the student body are minority students. To ensure that all students acquire the optimum benefits of a Stockton education, the college seeks to address students' diverse needs and interests while at the same time working to bring all students within a collective, harmonious community. At Stockton, the creation of a sense of college community and belonging to that community is viewed both as an essential part of a comprehensive retention strategy and as an essential support for the delivery of a high-quality liberal arts education.

Planning efforts, in keeping with the college mission, aim at creating a learning environment for students that encourages their active involvement. Moreover, the college's mission places the responsibility for participating actively in planning and managing personal development and growth both within and outside the classroom with the student. The college mission expects student initiative, supports student development, and values student involvement in Stockton's ongoing development.

The Role of Organizational Structure in Student Retention

On an institutional organization basis, the relationship between academic affairs and student services is one of the most important links to effective student retention. A good relationship between these areas fortifies the connection between the curriculum and extracurricular learning experiences. Academic affairs emphasizes the principal importance of the college's academic mission while supporting the student services emphasis on accomplishment of the institution's educational purpose through out-of-classroom learning experiences; the reverse is also true. Working together, they support an optimum learning environment for students.

At Stockton, academic affairs and student services work closely on a broad array of programs that enhance retention by helping students attain their goal within the institution's mission.

The infrastructures of academic affairs and student services have become similar over time. Each area has its own vice president with a concomitant set of deans (five for academic affairs and three for student services). The vice presidents, deans, and other staff members meet together frequently and cooperate across divisional lines on a significant number of student-oriented programs.

Two examples of joint efforts are the Summer Orientation Program and the funding of certain staff.

Summer Orientation Program

Approximately 700 freshmen and 500 transfer students participate in a summer orientation program designed to prepare them for actual course registration and to familiarize them with the college. Orientation includes seminars and programs designed to help entering students make a smooth transition to college life. Students meet with faculty advisors, student leaders, and college staff. A variety of student development workshops and sessions are available during the summer program as well as during the one-week orientation program prior to the commencement of fall and spring term classes.

The planning and implementation of all of the activities of this program are co-chaired by members from academic affairs and student services. Student leaders who work with the freshmen and transfer students use a "peer-to-peer" method. Student services staff meet with parents, and faculty interact with parents and students.

Prior to the actual orientation sessions, the student leaders, college staff, and faculty who will conduct the program undergo an intensive one-week training session. Because staff, students, and faculty are trained together, a level of comfort is established that is subsequently reflected to the incoming students. It continues the student-oriented theme, that the college's staff and faculty are accessible and visible and that student leaders have high stature and are valued.

Partnership among Student Senate, Student Services, and Academic Affairs to Jointly Fund Certain Staff Positions

There is a partnership among the student senate, student services, and academic affairs to jointly fund several key staff positions. Currently, four full-time staff positions are funded in this manner: evening and weekend program coordinator, administrative coordinator for student development, coordinator of intramurals and recreation, and coordinator for career services.

These are not the only staff positions in these areas, but having these four positions enables the college to use institutional funds to expand the number of faculty.

The student senate, student services, and academic affairs cooperate on the recruitment, hiring, and maintenance of the positions. It is truly unusual to have a student senate use student fees for the educational purpose of providing staff. More often, such fees are used primarily to provide extracurricular activities. This joint partnership, however, works very well.

The Role of Curricular Reforms in Retention Strategies

Academic interaction with faculty, opportunities for curricular choices, small class size, and interaction with other students in the classroom were some of the goals associated with our retention strategies. Examples of the programs used are:

Mentor Scholar Program

The Mentor-Scholar Program is a special opportunity that is offered each year to freshmen identified on the basis of particularly strong academic ability. Students enrolled in this program have the opportunity during their first year at Stockton to develop a one-on-one relationship with a faculty member that can last through the college years and to work on an independent study project of mutual interest.

Freshman Seminar Program

The freshman seminar program is designed to help students experience an appropriate or "first taste of" introduction to academic life.

Stockton has created freshman seminars that provide students with an early, authentic seminar experience in which they encounter the essential processes of academic discourse in the context of a full-credit academic course.

In the seminar, students develop and demonstrate the communication skills of speaking, listening, writing, and reading in a class small enough to allow the full expression of these capabilities. In addition to communication skills, students develop capacities for critical thinking, including reasoning and appreciation, and for teamwork on academic projects. Individual attention from the instructor is readily available.

All students entering Stockton as freshmen are required to enroll in a freshman seminar during their first term. Students may choose their freshman seminars from a range of courses in the various general studies categories. In many cases, students have their freshman seminar instructor as their preceptor (see below), which further strengthens this important bond.

The Preceptorial System

Stockton's educational philosophy is based on the concept that students should be challenged, motivated, and assisted through extensive faculty-student contact. This approach, combined with broad interdisciplinary flexibility, permits students to choose ways to pursue their goals.

In Stockton's preceptorial system, a matriculated student works closely and continuously with a faculty or staff preceptor to set educational goals, assess progress toward goals, and make adjustments as necessary. Students learn to build and implement programs of study which relate to what they wish to accomplish while meeting the overall goals of a liberal arts education.

A preceptor and preceptee work together to plan courses of study, explore career alternatives, and develop broad capacities for individual flexibility. The nature of the particular preceptor-student relationship is, by definition, variable, dependent always upon the differing personalities, abilities, and needs of those involved.

The Writing Program

The college offers a wide variety of writing courses to help students develop the skills necessary for success in college and crucial to many areas of professional and personal life after college. Writing-intensive (W1) courses focus primarily on the students' own writing while exploring particular subject matter. Writing across the curriculum (W2) courses are designed primarily to explore subject matter while using the students' writing as an important mode of learning and evaluation.

Mathematics-Across-the-Curriculum (MAC)

Stockton's Mathematics Across the Curriculum (MAC) program is designed to equip students with important quantitative skills that are useful throughout the academic disciplines. Throughout the undergraduate experience, a broad array of general studies and program courses provide rich encounters with mathematical ideas and their applications. With the MAC program, students are fortified with an additional knowledge base that opens new areas to them and assists them in understanding science and other math-related disciplines by ensuring that they will be able to master quantitative reasoning concepts.

An important feature of both the writing and MAC programs is that students build and use these skills in surprising contexts—e.g., writing in the sciences and math, in art, or in social work.

The MAC program is a cutting-edge approach to mathematics which recently won a National Science Foundation award for Advanced Institutional Reform. It also has received several major grants totaling more than $250,000.

Inclusion of Contributions of Minority/Ethnic Groups into the Curriculum

Several committees have worked on the campus and statewide to assist in infusing information about the contributions of various groups—African Americans, Hispanics, Asians—into the curriculum in a variety of ways.

The Role of Campus Community Life in Retention Strategies

Facilities

The college offers on-campus housing facilities that include garden-style apartments with private, exterior entrances and more traditional residence halls. Students, through the student senate, were actively involved in the design of the residential facilities. As a result, the facilities reflect some special options that are well liked by students—separate laundry facilities and small sleep areas with large lounge areas per room.

A community life environment that encourages communication, networking, and faculty, staff, and student contact works well to encourage student involvement. Student involvement in turn enhances student retention. In support of this idea, the student centers at Stockton are small scale by design and feature high traffic, multiple small communities, and easy interaction within the community. These facilities are:

- **Townsend Residential Life Center (TRLC)**
  The Townsend Residential Life Center is available to increase programming opportunities for residential living groups and to house functions provided by

the Office of Housing and Residence Life and the campus community. The TRLC contains a large multipurpose room with a kitchen, two smaller meeting rooms with kitchenettes, a microcomputer room, the Stock Market (convenience store), and an office which serves residence hall students during evenings and on weekends.

- **The Lakeside Center**

The Lakeside Center is a student life building located near the student apartment complex. The Towne Hall multipurpose room looks out over the lake and is equipped with an indoor/outdoor stage and sound and lighting equipment. The Lakeside Convenience Store and Pizza Parlor enable students to pick up groceries, a snack, or a meal which can be eaten at the center or taken to the student's apartment. Also included in the center is a meeting room, a computer lab with 20 work stations, and the Housing and Residence Life Office, which services apartment residents. The Lakeside Center provides cocurricular activities including dances, concerts, movies, speakers, banquets, and social and educational events for students.

- **College Center**

A 23,000 square-foot College Center is at the hub of the college. The lower level offers a variety of dining settings. The upper level includes a lounge, vending and reception areas, a conference room, office space for 53 student clubs and organizations, work areas for individual and group projects and student leaders, a radio station, the student newspaper, and a club/organization resource room with computers, a facsimile machine, typewriters, and a photocopier.

At the edge of the campus near the residence halls is a center which has a cafeteria accommodating meal-plan subscribers and seating 400. It also has information boards and seating and circulation areas. Located at the ground level is the Rathskeller, which serves snacks, soft drinks, beer, and wine. The upper level has two meeting rooms, the College Center offices, a spacious lounge, a television room, the Stockton student television office, and the yearbook office.

Special Programs

Several key special programs have been helpful in the retention of students at the college. They include:

The Declining Balance Card

Students have an alternative purchasing option called the Declining Balance. This program allows students to open an account with the cashier's office and to use their ID card to make purchases at the college bookstore or any of the campus food service areas. There are two options:

- **Unrestricted.** Money placed in this account can be used at any location on campus.

- **Restricted with added value.** Money placed in this account can only be spent in certain areas—all food service operations, including the convenience stores and pizzeria. When a purchase is made using these funds, the student receives a discount.

ULTRA—Undergraduate Learning Training and Awareness Program

This student development program provides students with the opportunity to participate in cocurricular workshops that contribute to their academic growth and personal and interpersonal development. Students who participate in any ULTRA program earn credits on their cocurricular transcripts.

Cocurricular Transcripts

The cocurricular transcript is an innovative student life initiative that was developed to document out-of-class learning experiences.

A cocurricular transcript is an official record of participation in any of the workshops included in the ULTRA program as well as participation in other Stockton-sponsored programs. As an official document, this transcript is used to complement a resume and academic transcript when applying to graduate schools and prospective employers.

Strategies for Retention of Commuter Students

A large proportion of commuter students do not live at home but reside in rental facilities near the college. Most of these students spend nearly as much time on campus as residential students. They study, eat, date, and participate in intramural and collegiate sports in addition to attending classes on campus. Retention efforts aimed at commuter students rest on including these students in the network and communication system of the college community.

The following are examples of support services provided for commuter students:

- **Staff**. The commuter coordinator works with commuter students' organizations and provides information about campus services to commuter students. The coordinator also plans orientation programs for new and traditional- and nontraditional-age commuters and acts as a contact point for students interested in carpooling.

- **Commuter Organization.** The commuter student organization represents the interests of commuter students on campus. The time and location of meetings are advertised on kiosks and gallery televisions. The organization meets to coordinate activities for commuting students, to discuss recommendations for policies and procedures affecting the population, and to bring issues before the student senate.

- **Carpooling.** A carpool directory was developed and is updated regularly.

- **Commuter Life Guidebook.** A *Guide for Off-Campus Commuter Living*, which offers helpful ideas for house hunting, lease preparation, moving, energy conservation, and security, is updated regularly.

Committee for the Enhancement of Commuter Student Life
The Committee for the Enhancement of Commuter Student Life provides the following programs and events:

- *Commuter Student Newsletter* published on a regular basis;

- *Handbook for Commuter and Nontraditional Students;*

- coordination of orientation programs and events for commuter and nontraditional students; and

- coordination of ULTRA programming series designed for commuter and nontraditional students.

Students in the Education Opportunity Fund (EOF) Program

The Educational Opportunity Fund Program is designed to meet the educational and financial needs of students whose potential for college may not be reflected in their grades and whose economic background makes it extremely difficult for them to pursue a college education without substantial financial aid.

As such, the EOF Program focuses on the academic development (e.g., intellectual skills and habits) of disadvantaged students. As part of the retention strategy for students in the EOF, the college places a great deal of emphasis on processes that increase confidence, develop social skills, and broaden horizons.

Two examples illustrate the college's programs and events for EOF students:

Summer Program Requirement (Academic Boot Camp)

Freshmen slated to attend the college term beginning in September are required to attend an Academic Boot Camp. This rigorous seven-week program is designed to strengthen students' adjustment to and preparation for college.

The summer program of courses, workshops, symposia, and cultural activities is intended to help students develop the self-discipline and social skills required to succeed not only in college, but after college as well.

A gala social ball is held in the fall to welcome EOF students to Stockton. The gala is cosponsored by the student senate and the president's office and is open to all students at the college for a nominal fee. Each EOF student and guest is invited as an honoree and is presented in a receiving line; each EOF student also is given a certificate to mark the occasion.

The gala social ball is a very well attended function and gets EOF students off to a good social start.

Policies Which Enhance Student Retention

Often, parents, other family members, and friends are very important in urging a student to graduate, particularly as they emphasize their desire to see the student graduate.

Students may march for spring or winter graduation if they are within one course of degree completion and provide evidence that they have registered for the required course.

Financial Aid and Class Attendance Policy

The college notifies all students receiving financial aid, including loans, that in order for them to remain eligible for all forms of aid, the college must be able to report to the U.S. Department of Education that the student is attending classes. Although instructors determine their own attendance policies for their courses, to meet federal requirements all instructors report to Student Records three times per term whether any student in their class did not attend at all during the previous four-week reporting period.

The college also has instituted an Emergency Loan Fund from which students may borrow up to $100 for emergencies.

Safety and Security Policy

Policies to ensure a safe and secure community environment result in student involvement and subsequent student retention.

The Stockton educational philosophy requires that individual members learn how to interact with one another and respect the rights of others. To this end, specific policies and guidelines have been established for providing a safe and secure community environment.

- **Confidentiality.** Policies regarding the handling of student information in a strictly confidential manner are enforced in accordance with federal, state, and college procedures and requirements.

- **Use of Substances** (*e.g., alcohol, smoking*). Students were actively involved in the development and implementation of policies dealing with substances. They helped write strict policies and stated the following:

> As an institution of higher education whose primary purpose is the pursuit of academic excellence, Stockton emphasizes development of the whole student, personally, socially, and educationally. It follows that with the academic mission at the forefront, cocurricular activities must enhance and not detract from academic pursuits of the community.
>
> This policy is based on the philosophy that community life at Stockton must demonstrate a respect for others as well as uphold the laws of the State of New Jersey.

Campus Grievance Procedure—Campus Hearing Board

It may seem odd to include a campus grievance procedure and safety and security measures under retention strategies. Yet a hostile and constantly changing environment with an unpredictable judicial system is very damaging to good retention. In fact, crime and violence on the campus increases attrition because the college often loses both the victims and the perpetrators.

Stockton takes seriously having a clearly defined Code of Conduct and an efficient and effective Hearing Board, which oversees reported infractions of the Code of Conduct.

- **Campus Hearing Board.** The regular membership of the Campus Hearing Board consists of students, faculty, and staff members.

- **Campus Hearing Board Panels.** There are four possible avenues which a hearing might take, depending on the factual circumstances involved: the Administrative Hearing, the Campus Hearing Board Panel Hearing, the Executive Committee Hearing, or a Special Administrative Hearing.

- **Campus Hearing Board Panel.** Regular panels generally hear cases when constituency-based representation on the hearing panel is available and particularly desirable. Examples include general violations of the college policy, such as disorderly conduct, theft, unauthorized entry, etc.

- **Composition.** When a student is accused of misconduct and appears before a hearing panel, the panel shall consist of three students, one faculty member, and one staff member; when a faculty member is accused of misconduct and appears before a hearing panel, the panel shall consist of three faculty members, one student, and one staff member; when a staff member is accused of misconduct and appears before a hearing panel, the panel shall consist of three staff members, one student, and one faculty member.

- **Sanctions.** Warning, reprimand, community service, probation, restitution, fine, suspension, dismissal, expulsion, and other sanctions may be imposed by the panel.

Misconduct that is motivated by intentional discrimination may result in the imposition of a more serious sanction.

Conclusion

Stockton's approach to student retention is comprehensive in scope rather than piecemeal. The relatively equal stature of academic affairs and student services provides the foundation from which jointly developed goals, objectives, programs, and services are formulated and implemented.

By using the special and unique skills and talents of faculty members and professional staff in a shared and cooperative effort, Stockton has been able to provide students with comprehensive, high-quality academic and educational support services, programs, and opportunities that lead to well-rounded personal growth, leadership, and development.

This sharing of institutional responsibility for the growth and development of the student both within and outside the classroom is a primary reason that Stockton has been successful in improving its student retention and graduation rates.

Academic Advising—
Key to Student Retention

Robert E. Glennen
President Emeritus
Emporia State University

The nation's public colleges and universities face challenges as never before. There is competition among prisons, health care, and education for state dollars. The public and policymakers are asking that higher education be more accountable. Students and their parents are asking for more services from colleges and universities yet are concerned that the costs are increasing. The critics of higher education—the taxpayers, legislators, administrative officials, higher education officers, staffs of charitable organizations, federal officials, and trustees and regents with direct judiciary responsibilities—believe that today's colleges and universities have become too set in their ways to change—that they resist the re-engineering and restructuring now going on in the corporate world. Public colleges and universities are competing with others who are "selling" education and credentials. Extension programs, corporate training programs, corporate colleges and universities, community learning centers, proprietary schools, and unaccredited institutions are all offering college courses, in many cases at times and locations that are more convenient to students. This is happening at the same time that campuses in some states are continuing to face decreasing state appropriations or are trying to make up for cuts in the early years of this decade. The amount of state funding per student is lower than at any time since the Great Depression. Because of fixed overhead costs which have to be spread over fewer students in case of declining or managed enrollments, presidents are forced to make difficult budgetary decisions. It is within this environment that presidents and chancellors must ensure the best campus climate possible, a climate where students are nurtured and encouraged to complete their education.

Although presidents and chancellors, some of whom have the authority to set tuition at their institutions, would rather not, it is often necessary to make up for declining state support by increasing tuition. The appropriations losses of the early 1990s, which continue in many states and which drove tuition up, had a negative effect on enrollment and limited access for many Americans. Promoting student persistence and academic success effectively enhances the retention of students and not only encourages them to continue with their education but also offsets the loss of tuition and funding revenue generated by fewer new students. Even with projected enrollment increases in the near future, as children of the baby boomers and new immigrants reach college age, retention remains integral to ensure that all students are given the benefit of postsecondary education.

Student retention is especially significant now that many institutions must retain students to help stabilize enrollments. One of the most effective retention tools is student advising. Studies have shown that students who receive effective academic advising tend to feel positive about the institution. Administrative support for advising has been found to positively affect student satisfaction, especially when CEOs communicate to the campus that advising is a high priority and that time spent advising students is an investment in the future of the student and the institution.

This is what makes the job of a college or university president so difficult. When tough decisions have to be made, it is often student counseling and advising services that have to be cut to save class offerings. One survey reviewing budget-cutting priorities discovered that 59 percent of all college presidents indicated that their first cuts would come from such support areas as student personnel, student affairs, counseling, and advising.[1] Cutting programs that promote retention is counterproductive in that it should be seen as a cost-saving activity.

Finances aside, Noel indicates that retention should not be the goal but is the result or byproduct of improved programs and services on our campuses.[2] Noel also points out a number of myths about retention: that retention means lowering standards; that dropouts are flunkouts; that students drop out primarily because of financial problems; and that retention is the responsibility primarily of student services, i.e., student success is someone else's concern.[3]

In reality, some of the major reasons for attrition are academic boredom; uncertainty about which major to pursue; transition/adjustment problems; lack of academic preparedness; and compatibility, i.e., lack of a good match between what the institution provides and what the student needs. Retention is highest at those institutions which create an atmosphere devoted to helping students achieve academic success and which provide a high-quality education. A review of retention literature contains many references to the importance of academic advising in increasing student retention. Habley states that the advisor is key in helping students make wise decisions relative to their educational goals.[4]

One successful model is a centralized advising system staffed by faculty using an intrusive approach. To be intrusive means to be concerned about the academic affairs of students.[5] In a faculty-based advising system, faculty assist students in course selection and scheduling, provide information about academic support services, monitor academic progress, check graduation requirements, and make referrals to other campus resources when appropriate.

In intrusive advising, the institution takes the initiative and is aggressive in calling students in for advising appointments. Intrusive advising is faculty based and is provided in a centralized location. Advisors use handbooks, catalogs, and campus referral resources.

The intrusive process is initiated each year with a full day of activity, as one of the programs for new students. It has the dual objectives of familiarizing students with the campus and advance-registering them for their fall schedule of classes. The program also includes a concurrent session for parents. Attendees are provided with an orientation to the residence halls, dining facilities, the Greek system, and recreational activities, and they meet with faculty advisors to work out the student's class schedule.

At the beginning of the academic year, students are asked to make an appointment at the advising center with an advisor from the student's intended major. This initial interview focuses on the student's past academic performance and the possible selection of a major and a degree program. Those whose previous academic performance was marginal are the first to be advised. Those who have received two or more mid-term deficiencies (D or F) after mid-term examinations are next in the sequence. They receive additional advising, referrals to academic support services, tutoring, or other assistance to help them improve their academic performance during the remainder of the semester. The end of the first semester is devoted to advance enrollment for the second semester.

The second semester begins with the Pre-enrollment Advising Day for students enrolling for the first time and focuses on high-risk matriculants as well as continuing students on academic probation. The next group to be seen by advisors are those individuals who have made the dean's list during the first semester. The students are told about the Honors Program and the various opportunities for honor students and are extended personal congratulations by the advisors for their fine academic performance. Spring semester closes with preregistration for summer school and advance registration for the next fall semester.

Additional components of the intrusive system include: at least two interviews with each student each semester; a readmission interview with students previously dismissed from the university; withdrawal interviews for students who plan to leave the university (to determine the reasons and to see if the university can provide any additional assistance to convince the individual to remain in school); and an early alert procedure in which professors, administrators, or residence hall staff who notice students having academic problems, personal problems, or excessive absences contact the advising center to address the problem before it becomes insurmountable.

Advisors quickly come to see themselves as student advocates whose primary goal is to serve students and to provide them with the best advice possible. Advisors rarely see themselves as protecting department enrollments.

Many faculty-based systems fail because faculty do not see academic advising as part of their contractual obligation; many feel uncomfortable in any setting except a classroom; many do not understand percentile ranks, test scores, or assessment data; and many are just not interested. Many faculty feel they receive no special recognition for advising. Crockett and Levitz, in a study of 754 institutions, found that (1) the majority of institutions have no formal recognition/ reward system for faculty who serve as advisors; (2) 75 percent do not consider advising effectiveness in promotion or tenure decisions; (3) few institutions provide in-service training for advisors; and (4) most institutions do not have an assessment system in place to evaluate the program or the individual advisors.[6] Unfortunately, this is still the scenario at many institutions today.

Faculty interact more frequently with students than any other group on the college campus. Faculty members reinforce the quality of the institution through the caliber of their instruction and the academic standards they impose. Many times, faculty members are the first to observe problems that students are having and to help them resolve those problems. They may also refer them to the Academic Advising Center, where someone more skilled in advising techniques can further assist them.

Even though retention is a campus-wide responsibility, faculty members often believe that retention is someone else's responsibility. A CEO has to ensure that everyone on the campus is committed to making students feel wanted and that they are willing to assist them in making a good adjustment and achieving academic success. Greenwood stated that nothing does more damage to the image of an institution than disgruntled, frustrated, or unhappy students who view the institution as a cold, uncaring, or unconcerned place.[7] When academic advising is perceived as effective, personal, and accurate, the image of the institution is always enhanced.

Faculty members establish credibility with students because of their contact with them in and out of the classroom. High-quality academic advising is based on the theory that faculty members can never know too much about their advisees. A high-quality advising program will collect data and share it with the faculty who do the advising so they may be appropriately informed about their advisees. Faculty must be convinced of the importance of student retention. One effective approach is to indicate to faculty that if enough students leave the institution through attrition, budget decreases will follow and faculty positions will have to be eliminated.

The problems resulting in attrition on a college campus do not emerge overnight and likewise will not be eliminated rapidly. It is essential that campuses develop a plan to address student retention; provide an administrative structure, budget, personnel, equipment, and facilities; and implement a strategic plan to bring about change. Academic advising can supply information about the institution which can facilitate good decision making and long-range strategic planning.[8] An advising program must demonstrate cost effectiveness or evidence that it is meeting the university mission, or it could be subject to downsizing or elimination.

Academic advising needs to be evaluated annually. Among the criteria assessed must be: the percentage of students persisting through graduation; freshman attrition; increases in enrollment, the number of credit hours, and grade point averages; an increase in the number of advising interviews; an increase in the number of counseling contacts; an increase in tutoring contacts; a decrease in the number of students on academic probation; a decrease in the number of withdrawals; and a decrease in the number of academic suspensions.

Computer-assisted advising is the best solution to one of the most common advising problems: the distribution of accurate academic information to advisors and students. Increased computer use and reduction in the size, cost, and operational complexity of computers have dramatically increased their use in higher education, particularly in providing advisors with up-to-date requirements for majors and graduation requirements.[9] Computers will never replace people as advisors, but they can assist advisors in monitoring academic requirements and the academic progress of their advisees. For example, advisors can use electronic mail to contact students and to share changes in policies or requirements. Degree audits can help students keep track of their academic progress.

One of the major resources used for referrals by academic advisors is the learning resource or learning assistance center. By referring students to a place where they can receive additional assistance in reading, writing, or mathematics, advisors can help them get over academic hurdles and progress more smoothly toward graduation. Learning programs facilitate academic development for students from the time of their orientation to the university until they graduate. Students profit from such resources and gain new knowledge, skills, and confidence. Formal interaction between academic advising programs and academic support personnel has proven important in maintaining and improving cooperation. When academic support personnel interact freely with academic advisors and participate in their staff meetings, they cultivate an environment of positive expectations for students. Academic support services become an effective bridge between academics and academic advising and enable students to achieve maximum performance.[10]

Another ingredient of a retention plan is the freshman seminar course. In this course, faculty members help students make a positive transition to the college setting, develop a sound academic program, and select career goals that are compatible with their aptitudes and interests. The teacher becomes the individual to whom students can go with their problems or questions; many times, this relationship lasts throughout the course of the student's undergraduate career. The goal of academic advising is to help students identify the goals they wish to attain and the courses they need to do so. Academic progress toward those goals is measured by credits earned and grades received. Forrest found that a comprehensive program of orientation and advising produced greater intellectual growth, persistence, and satisfaction among students.[11] Freshman orientation courses improve students' learning, general education, and satisfaction.

Students who attend college today—regardless of their ethnic background, age, or purposes for seeking education—face unprecedented personal, social, economic and educational challenges. Advising provides services which will help students persist to graduation. The effort to have an impact on retention on a college campus is never finished. It is an ongoing process—a goal that institutions must forever pursue!

Quetions from the Front . . .

Q. **What suggestions would you have for faculty on commuter campuses, especially those conducting classes using distance education techniques? How can they make vital student contacts and engage students in their educational experience?**

A. One way of looking at this question is to conceptually separate the data gathering and data integration segments of learning. The data gathering can be done by students over videotape, Internet listservs, the World Wide Web, or even at a traditional library or lecture. To enhance the data integration part of the educational experience, distance education courses should involve as much contact with faculty as possible. The greatest success and student satisfaction come when students are communicating with faculty and other students using listservs or e-mail over the Internet. It appears that the amount of interaction using this format is somewhat greater than that between faculty and students on campus.

Emporia State University has been very successful at rearranging our curriculum into the weekend-intensive class format. Students off campus find this more convenient and are able to build a sense of community. The faculty have found this a more effective delivery structure and have moved many of their on-campus courses to the same intensive format for pedagogical reasons. This, in turn, has been more convenient for our commuting students.

Some faculty report that the use of logs/journals which are interactive (these are turned in periodically and the faculty members provide comments/dialogue) have been helpful in personalizing instruction.

When using case study or problem approaches, we have found that making working groups of students from several instructional sites and having those problem or case groups work together over the Internet help the off-campus students feel that they are a part of the campus and bring a broader perspective to students on campus.

Q. **How can an institution break free of the common dilemma in which a handful of motivated and committed faculty and staff consistently bear the burden of multicultural education both inside and outside of the classroom? What are some proven approaches to this issue?**

A. Emporia State University has employed faculty development monies allocated for the purpose of bringing diversity into classroom instruction. These monies have been given to faculty who are starting to be interested in the area rather than to those who already have a reputation for their work in the area. We have also used the Regents Diversity Conference in the same way with some success. Analysis of this year's conference determined that next year's efforts should be to give strong preference to faculty who have not previously attended or shown an interest in the topic.

We have included an emphasis on diversity for new faculty by having this as the topic of discussion at one of our breakfasts. At this meeting, the expectation for all faculty members to be involved is shared with all new faculty.

The Teachers' College has had some success by focusing discussion and planning at the division level. Some divisions have focused on every faculty member targeting the same strategy (having conversations with students about diversity and its influence/impact on campus). Others have allowed/encouraged faculty to design and implement personal goals related to multicultural education. Having the focus at the division level enables faculty to get away from arguments like, "Well, that might work in the social sciences, but clearly there is no application that we can make in a statistics class."

In some divisions, faculty who care about this topic are identified as mentors and are assigned to assist and remind less-prepared faculty and also to mentor minority students. We have also created culturally diverse courses across the university.

Q. **With regard to language minority students, what have been the most successful strategies/programs to enhance education and retention?**

A. We have had more success with international students than with local students whose first language is Cambodian, Vietnamese, or Spanish. We do not encourage language minority students to room with people who speak their first language. We also have an international choir, and all students master the language better through singing.

Q. **The curriculum is the strongest statement an institution can make as its reason for being. What strategies or recommendations can you make for the academic leadership of the institution to provide a curriculum that is reflective of the population it serves?**

A. The university has convened advisory panels, committees, or groups of professionals in the appropriate fields in the Teachers' College, the School of Business, the School of Library and Information Management, and some divisions of the College of Liberal Arts and Sciences. These groups ensure that the education we provide meets the needs of those we serve.

We conduct regular surveys of employers and of graduates to assess the degree to which the curriculum is seen as useful and appropriate.

We have used accreditation groups as well as consultants to provide feedback.

To varying degrees, the divisions have met and discussed the feedback from the consultants and advisory groups. The process has resulted in many curriculum changes.

Q. How does a faculty member address the needs of individual students when he has hundreds of students in a single class?

A. There are very few classes on this campus that are that large. Even with our small class size, faculty use communications tools such as e-mail, which could be used at institutions with larger classes. In the few large classes, faculty members break them into smaller discussion groups so they can better acquaint themselves with the students.

Some faculty members assign "one-minute papers." Students are asked to spend one minute at the end of class writing whatever they have learned that day, or a position on an issue, or what questions they have. The faculty member reads these and comments on them the next day. Students report on course evaluations that this activity gives them a sense of personal attention even in a large class.

Q. How can members of institutions be challenged to engage in the personal, professional, and institutional change needed to construct effective learning environments?

A. The institution has to first provide the facilities or equipment for development. For example, the development of computer use was very slow until the university placed computers on all faculty members' desks and connected all to the token ring. Use also increased when the e-mail package (GroupWise™) was installed.

Providing physical facilities without training for faculty and staff is not sufficient. ESU implemented credit classes this year for faculty, and almost a third signed up for courses.

Relative to constructing effective learning environments, the School of Library and Information Management offered Internet and satellite courses. The university also sent a group of faculty to the SPRINT training center for a workshop.

The creation of a Teaching Enhancement Center for the university assisted faculty members in improving their teaching and technology skills. We have given released time and special stipends to faculty members who have worked on mediated courses. We are providing sabbaticals which are focused totally on addressing future instructional strategies.

Q. **How do we include disabled and learning disabled students as we strengthen, create, and recognize the importance of diversity on campus?**

A. Supporting a campus that celebrates its diversity requires that all qualified students feel welcome. To ensure this environment for disabled students, it must be agreed that everyone will work together proactively in order to provide equal educational opportunities. The major partners in this effort are the disabled student, teaching faculty and administration, and the Office of Disabled Student Services. Because disability-related information is considered by law to be private and protected, and because the disabled student is an adult, the student has the initial responsibility to identify himself/herself as having a disability, to document the disability, and to communicate to the other partners what accommodations are necessary. The Office of Disabled Student Services educates, facilitates, monitors, and advocates throughout this cooperative effort.

Emporia State University uses admissions personnel and relevant publications to recruit and initially welcome disabled students and to tell them how to access individualized services. The Office of Disabled Student Services then assumes an active role in helping the disabled student make the transition from applicant to successful student. A "can do" attitude relative to disabled students is also characteristic of the university. For example, students with learning disabilities may receive additional time to take exams, a quiet exam site, and readers or writers for exams. For disabled students whose preferred learning style is writing, a second set of notes is available. For those who learn best auditorially, a tape recorder can be used to record, play, and replay classroom discussions. Teaching styles may also vary; faculty may wear FM transmitters for hard-of-hearing students (the student wears the receiver and headphones); verbalize precisely what is written on the chalkboard or the computer screen for visually impaired students; or wait patiently for a speech-impaired student to complete a verbal response.

The services provided to disabled students are determined largely by individualized needs and personal choice. Disabled students have available to them all of the services that are available to non-disabled students. In addition, certain services are designed to meet specific disability-related needs. For example, students with physical disabilities have a lift device to help them in and out of the swimming pool. There is an adaptive physical education lab with individualized exercise, and electronic door openers are on all buildings. Students with learning disabilities can receive tutoring from Project Challenge. Students who are hard-of-hearing can use the sound amplification systems in the auditoriums. Students with visual impairments can use the closed-circuit magnification system located in the library to enlarge printed materials. There are other services that students can use regardless of disability. Examples include liaison with their rehabilitation services counselor, disability-related scholarships, specially designed and assigned computers, and letters written to professors requesting accommodations.

Q. How do we survey students' opinions about the university, including what they like or do not like?

A. The Office of Institutional Studies at ESU administers a series of written surveys to assess students' opinions on the university. These surveys include, but are not limited to, the following:

- New Freshman Student Survey
- New Transfer Student Survey
- End of Freshman Year Survey
- Graduating Senior Survey
- Non-Returning Student Survey
- Alumni Survey
- Campus Climate Survey

Efforts of other offices and organizations to assess students' opinions on the university include:

- The ACT Student Opinion Survey
- Associated Student Government Suggestion Box
- Exit Interview and Exit Interview Questionnaire
- Student Advising Center interviews and questionnaires that evaluate advising-related activities.

Q. Are students who are more goal oriented less likely to drop out? Do students simply drop out because they do not know what they want to major in?

A. Students with low pre-admission college test scores and those who have not chosen a major are more prone to drop out of college. Both of these factors reflect underlying reasons that a student may not be goal oriented or committed to making the effort required to be successful in college. Also, students who enroll late for college seem to lack persistence and commitment to college.

In general, students who are not goal oriented also require longer to graduate and may still be uncertain about their major after they have accumulated enough hours to achieve junior/senior standing. Students who are not goal oriented are less likely to be motivated to use the resources available to help them maximize their chances of being successful, e.g., academic support services, career counseling, etc. Having a goal to which one is committed is basic to a student's motivation to be successful in college.

Q. Discuss the use of mentoring programs and internships. Are they good strategies for retention? How are they set up?

A. There is a considerable body of knowledge which speaks to the relationship between positive role models and student behavior, including success in college. Federal student support service programs (Project Challenge on the ESU campus) provide peer mentors for project participants. Students who are employed to work in the program, as well as the director, serve as counselor and mentors for project participants. Data show that students who participate in such programs have higher retention rates than students who are not in the program.

ESU has a formal program for mentoring minority students. All faculty, staff, and administrators are invited to serve as mentors. Students are asked to participate, but they are not required to do so.

Graduate student interns work with students who are still undeclared after 30 hours and with those who are not doing well after mid-term grades. This is a good strategy for retention because it provides another opportunity for student volunteers to be involved.

The ESU counselor education program places interns in a number of student services offices. Other mentoring strategies include, but are not limited to, the following:

- Academic Support Services
- Nontraditional Student Program
- Single Parent Program
- Community Service Council
- International Student Program

Q. Does mandatory orientation enhance student retention? If so, how do you convince campus constituents that they should participate in this program?

A. Yes, orientation programs, both voluntary and mandatory, provide students with attitudes and information which will help them succeed. At ESU, new undergraduate students are required to participate in a New Student Program session. Students are informed about campus activities and services. Assuming that students retain some information and that being informed will help students adjust to campus, orientation programs should increase retention.

Communication is the most important factor in convincing campus constituencies that they should participate in such programs. Participation should be encouraged as an opportunity for campus constituents to make students aware of the services they offer and to encourage them to use such services. One way to demonstrate to faculty that orientation is important is to pay them for the time they devote to new student orientation programs.

Q. How do we achieve high academic expectations while at the same time integrating developmental courses and students into our credit classes?

A. Achieving high academic expectations would be enhanced if the faculty member teaching the developmental course were to coordinate or teach the credit course. This would ensure the best possible chance of student success without reducing the academic standards of credit courses. Providing supportive resources, e.g., math lab, reading lab, writing lab, etc., to help students develop the skills required to achieve in credit courses without lowering the level of credit courses is essential.

The rigors of an academic course should reflect the learning objectives and measurable goals of the course, not the caliber of the student taking the course. When students are challenged by the college curriculum, they invest more time and effort in learning activities.

Initial assessment of students' requisite knowledge will help ensure that they are prepared to perform in rigorous academic courses and that the quality of such courses will not be compromised. Some schools have initiated plus/minus grading programs to address the need for academic rigor and increased standards for academic performance.

Q. What is the correlation between faculty and staff morale and student retention?

A. The correlation between faculty and staff morale and student retention can be either positive or negative. For years, studies have reported that students who perceive that they "fit" the institution are more likely to persist than those who do not. One aspect of students feeling that they "fit" the institution is the quality of the interactions between students and faculty. Faculty and staff with nonchalant attitudes and who are disgruntled with the university are less likely to be motivated to engage in high-quality interactions with students, both within and outside the classroom. On the other hand, faculty and staff with high morale are more likely to engage in high-quality interactions with students. The CEO of the campus plays a significant role in establishing an atmosphere on campus that encourages student success and persistence toward academic goals.

Notes

[1]Moore, K. M. *Leaders in Transition*. Washington, DC: American Council on Education, 1983.

[2]Noel, L., R. Levitz, & D. Saluri (Eds.). *Increasing Student Retention: Effective Programs and Practices for Reducing the Dropout Rate*. San Francisco: Jossey-Bass, 1985.

[3]Ibid.

[4]Habley, W. "Academic Advising: The Critical Link in Student Retention," *NASPA Journal*, 28 (4), (1981): 45–50.

[5]Glennen, R. E. "Intrusive College Counseling," *College Student Journal*, 9, (1975): 2–4.; Glennen, R. E. "Effective Outcome Measures of Intrusive Advising Programs," in J. E. Roueche (Ed.). *A New Look at Successful Programs*. San Francisco: Jossey-Bass, 1983, pp. 59–71.; Glennen, R. E., & D. M. Baxley. "Reduction of Attrition through Intrusive Advising," *NASPA Journal*, 22, (1985): 10–15.; Glennen, R. E. "Intrusive Advising: Innovative Anecdote for Attrition," *Journal of Counseling and Human Service Professions*, 5, (1991): 34–41.

[6]Crockett, D. S., & R. Levitz. *A National Survey of Academic Advising: Final Report*. Iowa City, IA: American College Testing Program, 1983.

[7]Greenwood, J. D. "Academic Advising and Institutional Goals: A President's Perspective," in R. B. Winston, Jr., T. K. Miller, S.C. Ender, T. J. Grites & Associates. *Developmental Academic Advising*. San Francisco: Jossey-Bass, 1984, pp. 64–88.

[8]Farren, P. J. "Fiscal Affairs," in R. E. Glennen & F. N. Vowell (Eds.). *Academic Advising as a Comprehensive Campus Process*. NACADA, 1985, pp. 19–23.

[9]Kramer, G. L., & M. McCauley. "High Tech and High Touch: Integrating Information Technology in the Advising Process," in R. E. Glennen & F. N. Vowell (Eds.). *Academic Advising as a Comprehensive Campus Process* NACADA, 1995, pp. 27–33.

[10]Browne, G., R. Cunningham, C. Gruber & R. McGuire. "Academic Advising and Intercollegiate Athletics," in R. E. Glennen & F. N. Vowell (Eds.). *Academic Advising as a Comprehensive Campus Process* NACADA, 1995, pp. 69–73.

[11]Forrest, A. "Creating Conditions for Student and Institutional Success," in L. Noel, R. Levitz, & D. Saluri (Eds.). *Increasing Student Retention*. San Francisco: Jossey-Bass, 1985.

Bibliography

Browne, G., R. Cunningham, C. Gruber & R. McGuire. Academic Advising and Intercollegiate Athletics," in R. E. Glennen & F. N. Vowell (Eds.). *Academic Advising as a Comprehensive Campus Process* NACADA, 1995, pp. 69–73.

Crockett, D. S., & R. Levitz. *A National Survey of Academic Advising: Final Report.* Iowa City, IA: American College Testing Program, 1983.

Farren, P. J. "Fiscal Affairs," in R. E. Glennen & F. N. Vowell (Eds.). *Academic Advising as a Comprehensive Campus Process.* NACADA, 1985, pp. 19–23.

Forrest, A. "Creating Conditions for Student and Institutional Success," in L. Noel, R. Levitz, & D. Saluri (Eds.). *Increasing Student Retention.* San Francisco: Jossey-Bass, 1985.

Glennen, R. E. "Effective Outcome Measures of Intrusive Advising Programs," in J. E. Roueche (Ed.). *A New Look at Successful Programs.* San Francisco: Jossey-Bass, 1983, pp. 59–71.

Glennen, R. E. "Intrusive College Counseling." *College Student Journal,* 9 (1975): 2–4.

Glennen, R. E., & D. M. Baxley. "Reduction of Attrition through Intrusive Advising," *NASPA Journal,* 22 (1985): 10–15.

Glennen, R. E. "Intrusive Advising: Innovative Anecdote for Attrition," *Journal of Counseling and Human Service Professions,* 5 (1991): 34–41.

Greenwood, J. D. "Academic Advising and Institutional Goals: A President's Perspective," in R. B. Winston, Jr., T. K. Miller, S.C. Ender, T. J. Grites, & Associates. *Developmental Academic Advising.* San Francisco: Jossey-Bass, 1984, pp. 64–88.

Habley, W. "Academic Advising: The Critical Link in Student Retention," *NASPA Journal,* 28 (4) (1981): 45–50.

Kramer, G. L., & M. McCauley. "High Tech and High Touch: Integrating Information Technology in the Advising Process," in R. E. Glennen & F. N. Vowell (Eds.). *Academic Advising as a Comprehensive Campus Process.* NACADA, 1995, pp. 27–33.

Moore, K. M. *Leaders in Transition.* Washington, DC: American Council on Education, 1983.

Noel, L. (Ed.) *Reducing the Dropout Rate.* San Francisco: Jossey-Bass, 1978.

Noel, L., R. Levitz, & D. Saluri (Eds.). *Increasing Student Retention: Effective Programs and Practices for Reducing the Dropout Rate.* San Francisco: Jossey-Bass, 1985.

Retention Strategies
for Campus Success

Rosario Martinez
Executive Director
George Washington Carver Center
North Harris College

The following questions were asked during a live AASCU/PBS videoconference, "Retention Strategies for Campus Success." There wasn't time to answer them as part of the live event, but AASCU asked Dr. Martinez, an expert currently working on retention efforts, to provide answers for this publication.

Q. **In terms of language, what are some successful strategies/programs that have enhanced education and retention?**

A. It is important to understand that each individual brings something different when they come to college, and that "something" must not be lost. Do not label students. Let them express their humanity. We live in a global village; therefore, we must use global education. Remember that if a student has an accent, we do not want to contribute to the student's belief that "something is wrong with me." Faculty must be creative, tolerant, accommodating, and flexible. We have to use adaptive teaching methods and understandable instruction with language-minority students. Collaborative learning and teaching have been successful.

Q. What models exist for community colleges to improve retention rates in urban, metropolitan areas?

A. Models must create an environment that encourages and nurtures student success. It is critical that the model promote understanding and acceptance of diversity. Models that include strategies that translate retention into academic excellence are good. As the late former Congresswoman Barbara Jordan (featured in the videoconference) so eloquently stated, we must enrich students' academic achievement; help them realize their potential, their dreams. Having high expectations for student learning is part of academic excellence.

- Several successful retention programs provide students with opportunities to receive academic or educational support, e.g., tutoring, learning labs, computer-assisted instruction, computer training and access, financial aid. One community college even rents laptop computers for students to check out from the library so they can complete their assignments. Federal financial aid pays the computer rental fee.

- Models that provide financial assistance have been successful. For the third year at North Harris College, Carver Center, the Swalm Foundation has provided tuition, books and fees, and child care to qualifying students. Most of the students participating in the program are first-generation college enrollees, black American women who could not obtain any other form of financial assistance to attend college. Many also have small children who need care while they attend classes. The program has a 95 percent retention rate.

- There are numerous model programs that include mentoring or that provide students with internship experiences. Mentoring programs and internships are excellent strategies for retention. Successful programs have clear goals, objectives, expectations, activities, and desired outcomes. These programs vary from leadership training for students to structured faculty/student, student/student, business person/student programs. Adopt-a-school or -college or -university mentoring programs sometimes involve students and members of a church or business.

- Internships typically involve a structured learning experience for the student. The student pairs with a business mentor or a particular unit of business or industry that matches the student's interest. Student internships with congressmen or the legislature are popular components of government courses.

- Models that include curricula that reflect the contributions of women and ethnic minorities for the purpose of creating a climate of inclusion have increased retention. Integrating diversity in a classroom may be accomplished by something as simple as involving a visiting professor who represents a different group.

- Programs that require a student to "bond" with the college increase retention. Summer bridge programs to help academically disadvantaged high school seniors prepare for college often become a strong bonding experience for students.

- Barbara Jordan urged us to commit to educating as well as graduating students. Public community colleges are open door institutions where a student's educational objective may be fine-tuning job skills by taking a computer course; graduation may not be the student's goal. Success is not equal to graduation for all community college students; for example, a student who transfers, completes a program of study, or meets her own educational objective is successful. Therefore, tracking and longitudinal programs that adequately and systematically measure individual student success in college by using completion of individual educational objectives increase retention if some method of rewarding the student is incorporated.

- Programs that eliminate labels are successful. They can include activities that encourage students to bring their total self to campus.

- Seminars, workshops, or lectures that facilitate dialogue on sensitive issues and encourage interaction between faculty members and other faculty members, students and faculty members, and students and other students increase retention. An effective model program explored the questions: what does affirmative action REALLY mean, what does it mean to you, and what was it designed to mean? These questions were discussed in an open setting by ethnic minority and nonminority students, women, faculty members, and administrators.

- The literature shows that bridge programs can increase retention. Many different models exist. Some programs are designed for high school students who remediate during the summer in preparation for college. There are also early intervention programs. Other bridge programs are essentially strategies that weave the seamless web of higher education from community college to university. These programs involve articulation agreements, joint admissions agreements, or transfer guarantees.

- School-to-work programs which include internships, cooperative agreements between institutions and the business and industry community, comprehensive career counseling, and placement programs help increase retention.

- Transfer centers or programs that improve communication between the community college and the university for the purpose of facilitating the transfer of students increase retention.

Q. **To follow up on Dr. Vincent Tinto's recommendations to faculty, what suggestions does the panel have for faculty on commuter campuses and those conducting classes using distance education techniques to make those vital student contacts and engage students in their educational experience?**

A. It is important to first define distance education. Traditional distance learning, where a faculty member meets with students a prescribed number of times during the semester, does not encourage contact with students. Even though a student may have elected this mode of learning because there is minimal contact, it may not be the best situation in which that student can learn. Even in the traditional distance education model, faculty members can still follow good practices. The videoconference panel suggested, and I agree, that instructors should:

- hold high expectations for learning;

- use inclusive curricula, i.e., use Chinese, Native American, and European perspectives as part of a central or core curricular experience;

- provide appropriate educational and academic support, i.e., tutoring, learning labs; and

- provide students with frequent and constructive feedback (using the telephone or other technologies to check student progress can be helpful).

The concept of outside classroom learning is important in any type of distance learning. Faculty can still incorporate some method of individualized, personalized communication with students. They can be mentors and advocates over different types of communication lines (e.g., telephone, fax). Students should be contacted individually outside the learning environment as frequently as necessary. Staff, other students, and peer advisors can also provide assistance in contacting students. Asking about a student's progress by whatever method a faculty member chooses can contribute to the student's sense of connection to the learning environment.

Two-way, interactive, real-time distance learning can be similar to a traditional learning environment, and the previously mentioned recommendations are still applicable.

Q. How can an institution break free of the common dilemma in which a handful of motivated and committed faculty members and staff consistently bear the burden of multicultural education, both inside and outside the classroom? What are some proven approaches to this issue?

A. It is first important to examine the institution's mission. Is faculty involvement part of the mission statement? Is multicultural education part of the mission's role and scope? Do the goals and outcomes as outlined in the strategic plan incorporate multicultural education? Do these include faculty involvement in the process? Do the governing board, trustees, and CEO believe that these activities are part of the institution's culture, part of the infrastructure, and central and endemic to the mission?

In other words, if multicultural education is in an institution's mission statement and strategic planning process, faculty and staff will participate because they are required to and rewarded for it. They would be evaluated formally on behavior and actions that support multicultural education. It would then be important to use an adequate faculty reward system, whether individual or departmental. Individual rewards could include released time, recognition, money, priority in obtaining technology, balancing activities with credit hour workload, or other incentives. Departmental rewards can be the acquisition of more faculty, staff, equipment or supplies, adjustment of workload for all faculty in the department, or rewards that would be beneficial to the entire department.

Q. The curriculum sends a strong message about the institution's mission. What strategies or recommendations can the panel make for the academic leadership of the institution to provide a curriculum that is reflective of the population it serves?

A. The institution's leadership must promote societal realities and goals that underscore the fact that we live in a global village. The mission, goals, and expectations of the institution need to go beyond the development of the individual and support the common good to be an effective learning environment. In our global village, the significant educational experience is multidimensional and multifaceted, not ethnocentric.

About the Authors

Ruben Armiñana

Dr. Armiñana became the sixth president of Sonoma State University (Calif.) in 1992. He is former president of the Western College Association and held administrative positions and faculty appointments at California State Polytechnic University, Pomona and Tulane University before coming to Sonoma State. While at Sonoma State, Dr. Armiñana has been successful in furthering the academic and instructional offerings of the university despite yearly budget cuts. He created Educational Mentoring Teams, which improved the retention and graduation of students. He instituted the Assured Access Program, requiring 24-hour access to personal computing for students, and successfully integrated the university with the surrounding community. He has a Ph.D. in political science from the University of New Orleans, an M.A. from the University of Texas at Austin, and an A.A. from Hill College (Texas). A professor of political science, Dr. Armiñana teaches a course at Sonoma State every year.

Pamela G. Arrington

Dr. Arrington is a senior staff specialist with the Division of Planning and Academic Affairs at the Maryland Higher Education Commission. Her responsibilities include policy analysis, academic program review—including statewide review of teacher education programs—minority education policy and programs, and workforce training initiatives. From 1993 until 1996, she directed the American

Association of State Colleges and University's National Retention Project. Before taking the Maryland position, she was a professor of human resources development at Bowie State University (Md.). She earned a Ph.D. in education and social psychology from George Mason University (Va.) and has an M.A. in counseling from the University of Michigan and a B.A. in psychology from Spelman College (Ga.).

Drew M. Calandrella

Drew Calandrella is associate vice president for Student Academic Services at Sonoma State University (Calif.). He provides leadership for the retention unit on campus, which includes the Financial Aid Office, Residential Life, Academic Advising, Career Development, new student orientation, testing services and the Disability Resource Center. He has been in higher education administration for most of his career. He has a M.Ed. and B.A. from Trenton State College.

Don Farish

Dr. Farish was born in Winnipeg, Canada, and earned a B.S. degree in zoology at the University of British Columbia. He has an M.S. in entomology from North Carolina State University, a Ph.D. in biology from Harvard University, and a J.D. from the University of Missouri. He was on the faculty of the University of Missouri for 11 years, before relocating to the University of Rhode Island for four years as an assistant, then an associate dean in the College of Arts and Sciences. Farish came to Sonoma State University in 1983 as the dean of the School of Natural Sciences. In 1990 he was named vice president for academic affairs. He is the author of three textbooks and numerous publications in science and higher education.

Vera King Farris

Dr. Farris has been president of the Richard Stockton College of New Jersey since 1983. In recognition of her professional achievements and contributions to higher education and society, *New Jersey Woman* magazine chose her as its 1992 woman of the year. She was chair of the board of directors of the American Association of State Colleges and Universities in 1997 and is past president of the Middle States

Association of Colleges and Schools. She received a Hero in Public Housing award from the U.S. Department of Housing and Urban Development in 1996 and was a Washington Center 1992 Education Award winner for her leadership in education. Dr. Farris was academic vice president at Kean College of New Jersey and vice provost for academic affairs at the State University of New York–Brockport before coming to Richard Stockton. She earned a Ph.D. in parasitology and an M.S. in zoology and parasitology from the University of Massachusetts and has a B.S. in biology from Tuskegee University.

Robert E. Glennen Jr.

Dr. Glennen is president emeritus and a Jones Distinguished Professor at Emporia State University (Kans.), having served as president from 1984 until 1997. He has published widely on academic advising and undergraduate guidance. He was the recipient of the National Academic Advising Association's Award of Excellence for contributions to the field and a recipient of an award by the American Association of Colleges for Teacher Education for outstanding presidential support of teacher education. He chaired the American Association of State Colleges and Universities' Commission on Teacher Education and has served as a consultant on academic advising, student retention, and teacher education. He has a Ph.D. in counseling from the University of Notre Dame and an M.Ed. and A.B. from the University of Portland (Ore.).

Joel M. Jones

Dr. Jones has been president of Fort Lewis College (Colo.) since 1988, following 19 years at the University of New Mexico, where he was chair of the American Studies Program and held several administrative positions, including vice president for administration, planning, and student affairs. He earlier chaired the American Studies Program at the University of Maryland. He has published and spoken on inclusion and access issues as well as environmental studies, educational planning and program development, and American social and intellectual history. He received his B.A. from Yale University, his M.A. from Miami University of Ohio, and his Ph.D. at the University of New Mexico.

Rosario Martinez

Dr. Rosario Martinez is executive director of the G.W. Carver Center of North Harris College (Texas). The center is a partnership among the Aldine Independent School District, North Harris College, and the Houston business community developed to teach credit and community education classes to an underserved inner-city community. Dr. Martinez was director of Educational Opportunity Planning, the state plan for access and retention for African American and Hispanic faculty and students. She also led several retention projects to facilitate transfer of students from community colleges to universities. She writes extensively and has lectured internationally on student retention issues. She earned the Ph.D. and M.S. degrees from the University of North Texas at Denton and has a bachelor's degree from the University of Texas at El Paso.

Kenneth E. Redd

Mr. Redd is research associate for the American Association of State Colleges and Universities. Previously, he served as a research and policy analyst for the National Association of Independent Colleges and Universities. His areas of research interest and experience include minority enrollments and academic achievement, student financial aid, and institutional finances and degree completions. He has published articles on trends in minority college graduates and educational attainment. He has a B.A. from Tufts University and an M.A. from the University of Minnesota.

Richard C. Richardson Jr.

Dr. Richardson is a noted author of books and articles on effective learning environments and a member of the National Advisory Committee of the AASCU/ Sallie Mae National Retention Project. He is currently a professor in the Division of Education Leadership and Policy Studies at Arizona State University and is a senior researcher with the California Higher Education Policy Center. He serves as a consultant to the College Board on issues of equity and the academy. Dr. Richardson was the founding president of Northampton County Area Community College and served as associate director of the National Center for Postsecondary Governance. He holds a Ph.D. in education administration from the University of Texas and has an M.A. from Michigan State University and a B.S. in education from Castleton State College (Vt.).

Joyce A. Scott

Dr. Scott is vice president for academic and international programs at the American Association of State Colleges and Universities. She has written extensively about nontraditional education, faculty compensation, and academic policy. She manages the AASCU/Sallie Mae National Retention Project, as well as offices of rural, urban and international programs. She is involved in directing work and projects at the national level that address distance education, faculty recruiting, retention and diversity, accreditation and assessment, and strategic planning. Before coming to AASCU, Dr. Scott was executive vice president for academic affairs and dean of faculties at Wichita State University (Kans.). Dr. Scott served as provost and vice president for academic affairs at the State University of New York College at Potsdam and held various administrative positions at the University of Wyoming. She holds a Ph.D. in romance languages from Duke University, an M.A. in French from the University of Virginia, and a bachelor's degree in French and English from the University of Connecticut.

Mary Aleta White

Ms. White is a doctoral student in higher education administration at Arizona State University (ASU). She is currently working with Dr. Richard C. Richardson Jr. in the Division of Education Leadership and Policy Studies. Previously, she worked with the American Association of State Colleges and Universities as a researcher for the AASCU/Sallie Mae National Retention Project. White has a master's degree in fine arts in creative writing from Arizona State University and a bachelor's degree in English from Florida State University. She was a program coordinator for the Coalition to Increase Minority Degrees at ASU and was assistant to the chair of the ASU Committee on African American and African Studies after teaching first-year composition.

Bibliography

Bibliography Prepared by
Vincent Tinto
Syracuse University

Mary Aleta White
Arizona State University

Aitken, N." College Student Performance, Satisfaction, and Retention," *Journal of Higher Education*, 53 (1982): 32-50.

Allen, W. R., E. G. Epps, and N. A. Haniff (Eds.). *African American Students in Predominantly White and in Historically Black Public Universities*. Albany, NY: State University of New York Press, 1991.

Angelo, T., and P. Cross. *Classroom Assessment Techniques: A Handbook for College Teachers*. San Francisco: Jossey-Bass, 1993.

Astin, A. W. *Four Critical Years*. San Francisco: Jossey-Bass, 1977.

_____. *Minorities in Higher Education: Recent Trends, Current Prospects, and Recommendations*. San Francisco: Jossey-Bass Publishers, 1982.

_____. *Preventing Students from Dropping Out*. San Francisco: Jossey Bass, 1975.

_____. *What Matters in College*. San Francisco: Jossey-Bass, 1993.

Astin, H.S., and C. P. Burciaga. *Chicanos in Higher Education Programs and Attainment*. Los Angeles: Higher Education Research Institute, 1982.

Attinasi, L. "Getting In: Mexican Americans' Perceptions of University Attendance and the Implications for Freshman Year Persistence," *Journal of Higher Education*, 60 (1989): 247-77.

Bagayoko, D., and E. Kelley. "The Dynamics of Student Retention: A Review and a Prescription." *Education*. 115 (1994) (1).

Baird, L. L. (Ed.). *Increasing Graduate Student Retention and Degree Attainment*. San Francisco: Jossey-Bass, 1993.

Baird, L. L. "Studying Graduate Student Retention and Degree Attainment: Resources for Researchers." *New Directions for Institutional Research*, 80 (1993): 81.

Beal, P. and L. Noel. *What Works in Student Retention*. Iowa City: The American College Testing Program, 1980.

Beal, P., and E. Pascarella. "Designing Retention Interventions and Verifying Their Effectiveness," in E. Pascarella (Ed.). *Studying Student Attrition.* San Francisco: Jossey-Bass, 1982.

Bennet, C., and J. Bean. "A Conceptual Model of Black Student Attrition at a Predominantly White University," *Journal of Educational Equity and Leadership,* 4(3)(1984): 173-188.

Blanc, R. A., L. E. Debuhr, and D.C. Martin. "Breaking the Attrition Cycle: The Effects of Supplemental Instruction on Undergraduate Performance and Attrition," *Journal of Higher Education,* 54 (1983): 80-90.

Boger, Ruth E., K. M. Duwve, and L. A. Bankey. "Involving Graduate Assistants in Student Retention Efforts," *College and University.* 69(2) (1994): 100.

Bonwell, C., and J. Eison. "Active Learning: Creating Excitement in the Classroom," *ASHE-ERIC Higher Education Reports.* Washington DC: George Washington University, 1991.

Borkowski, F. T. "The University President's Role in Establishing an Institutional Climate to Encourage Minority Participation in Higher Education," *Peabody Journal of Education,* 66(1) (1988): 32-45.

Boulard, G. "Retention: Rates and Practices Vary From Campus to Campus," *Black Issues in Higher Education,* 27 January, 1994; 32-35.

Boudreau, C. A., and J. D. Kromrey. "A Longitudinal Study of the Retention and Academic Participants in Freshman Orientation Course," *Journal of College Student Development,* 35(6) (1994): 444.

Boylan, H. R., D. P. Saxon, A. L. Corum, A. and J. R.White. "Research Based Approaches to Promoting Minority Retention Through TRIO Programs," *Journal of the National Council of Education Opportunity Associations,* 1995, 28-32.

Boylan, H. R., D. P. Saxon, J. R. White, and A. Erwin. "Retaining Minority Students through Developmental Education," *Research in Developmental Education,* 11(3) (1994).

Brown, S. P. "Images of Me: A Model to Promote Retention of Black Female Students on Predominantly White Campuses," *Journal of College Student Development,* 35(2) (1994): 150.

Cabrera, A. F., A. Nora, and M. B. Castaneda. "College Persistence: Structural Equations Modeling Test of an Integrated Model of Student Retention," *The Journal of Higher Education,* 64(2) (1994): 123.

Cabrera, A. F., J. O. Stampen, and W. L. Hansen. "Exploring the Effects of Ability to Pay on Persistence in College," *The Review of Higher Education,* 13 (1990): 303-36.

Carreathers, K. R., L. Beekmann, and W. L. Nelson."Programmatic Components of Three Exemplary Retention Programs for Regularly Admitted Students of Color Are Described," *New Directions for Student Services*, 74 (1996): 35

Chickering, A. W. *Commuting Versus Resident Students*. San Francisco: Jossey-Bass, 1974.

Christie, N. G., and S. M. Dinham.. "Institutional and External Influences on Social Integration in the Freshman Year," *Journal of Higher Education*, 62 (1991): 412-436.

Cleave, S. L. "Residence Retention: Reasons Students Choose to Return or Not to Return," *College Student Journal*, 30(2) (1996): 187.

Clewell, B. C., and M. S. Ficklen. *Improving Minority Retention in Higher Education: A Search for Effective Institutional Practices*. Princeton: Educational Testing Service, 1986.

Cooper, J. L., and E. R. Mueck "Student Involvement in Learning: Cooperative Learning and College Instruction," *Journal of Excellence in College Teaching*, (1) (1990): 68-76.

Cosgrove, T. J. "The Effects of Participation in a Mentoring-Transcript Program on Freshmen," *Journal of College Student Personnel*, 27 (1986):119-24.

Creamer, D. "Educational Advising for Student Retention," *Community College Review*, 7(1980):11-18.

Credle, J. O., and G. J. Dean. " A Comprehensive Model for Enhancing Black Student Retention in Higher Education," *Journal of Multicultural Counseling and Development*, 19(4) (1991): 158.

Cross, P. and H. Astin. "Factors Affecting Black Students' Persistence in College," in G Thomas (Ed.). *Black Students in Higher Education: Conditions and Experiences in the 1970s*. Westport: Greenwood Press, 1981.

Crouse, R. "Peer Network Therapy: An Intervention with the Social Climate of Students in Residence Halls," *Journal of College Student Personnel*, 23 (1982): 105-8.

Dale, P. M., and T. Zych. "A Successful College Retention Program," *College Student Journal*, 30(3) (1996): 354.

Dodd, J. M., F. M. Garcia, and J. R. Nelson. "American Indian Student Retention," *NASPA Journal*, 33(1) (1995): 72.

Dukes, F., and G. Gaither. "A Campus Cluster Program: Effects on Persistence and Academic Performance," *College and University*, 59 (1984):150-66.

Dunston, F. M. *Review of the Literature: Black Student Retention in Higher Education Institutions*. Chapel Hill, NC: Research and Evaluation Associates, 1983. (ERIC Document Reproduction No. 228 912).

Eddy, J., J. Cochran, and C. Haney. "College Student Retention Studies and Strategies," in *College Student Personnel Development, Administration, and Counseling.* J. Eddy, J. Dameron, and D. Borland, (Eds.). Washington, DC: University Press of America, 1980.

Edmonds, G. I. "Needs Assessment Strategy for Black Students: An Examination of Stressors and Program Implications," *Journal of Non-White Concerns,* 12 (1984):48-56.

Endo, J. J., and R L. Harpel "The Effect of Student-Faculty Interaction on Students' Educational Outcomes," *Research in Higher Education,* 16 (1982): 115-35.

Endo, J. J. and T. Bittner. *Using an Integrated Marketing and Attrition Model from a Student Information System to Examine Attrition after One Year. Office of Academic Planning and Budget,* University of Colorado, Boulder, 1984.

Erickson, B L., and D. W. Strommer. *Teaching College Freshmen.* San Francisco: Jossey-Bass, 1991.

Feldman, M. J. "Factors Associated with One-Year Retention in a Community College," *Research in Higher Education,* 34 (4) (1993): 503.

Fidler, P. P., and M.A. Godwin. "Retaining African-American Students Through the Freshman Seminar," *Journal of Developmental Education,* 17(3) (1994).

Fleming, J.E. "Blacks in Higher Education to 1954: A Historical Overview," in *Black Students in Higher Education,* G. E. Thomas, (Ed.), Westport, Connecticut: Greenwood Press, 1981, pp. 11- 17.

Fleming, J.E. *Blacks in College.* San Francisco: Jossey-Bass, 1985..

Gablenick, F., J. MacGregor, R. Matthews, and B. Smith "Learning Communities: Creating Connections Among Students, Faculty, and Disciplines," *New Directions for Teaching and Learning,* No. 41. San Francisco: Jossey-Bass, 1990.

Giles-Gee, H. F. "Increasing the Retention of Black Students: a Multimethod Approach," *Journal of College Student Development,* 30(3) (1989): 196.

Giordano, F. G. "Evaluation as Empowerment: Using Evaluation Strategies to Improve Retention of Regularly Admitted Students of Color," *New Directions for Student Services,.* 74 (1996): 69.

Glennen, R. E., and D.M. Baxley. "Reduction of Attrition through Intrusive Advising," *NASPA Journal,* 22 (1985): 1014.

Gold, J. M.. "An Intergenerational Approach to Student Retention," *Journal of College Student Development,* 36(2) (1995): 182.

Goodsell, A., M. Maher, and V. Tinto. *Collaborative Learning: A Sourcebook for Higher Education.* University Park: The National Center on Postsecondary Teaching, Learning, and Assessment, 1992.

Gosman, E. J., B. A. Dandrige, M. T. Nettles, and A. R. Thoeny. "Predicting Student Progression: The Influence of Race and Other Student and Institutional Characteristics on College Student Performance," *Research in Higher Education*, 18(2) (1983).

Habley, W. R. " Academic Advising: The Critical Link in Student Retention," *NASPA Journal*, 18 (1981): 45-50.

Hearn, J. C. "Determinants of College Students' Overall Evaluations of Their Academic Programs," *Research in Higher Education*, 23 (1985): 413-37.

Henderson, J. C.:"Minority Student Retention," *New Directions for Community Colleges*, 74 (1991): 47.

Herndon, S. "The Impact of Financial Aid on Student Persistence," *Journal of Student Financial Aid*, 14 (1984): 3-9.

Hossler, D. *Enrollment Management: An Integrated Approach*, New York: College Entrance Examination Board, 1984.

Hossler, D., (Ed.) *Evaluating Student Recruitment and Retention Programs*. San Francisco: Jossey-Bass, 1991.

Isaac, P. D. "Measuring Graduate Student Retention," *New Directions for Institutional Research*. 80 (1993): 13.

Iwai, S. I., and W. Churchill. "College Attrition and the Financial Support System of Students," *Journal of Research in Higher Education*, 17 (1981): 105-13.

Jacobi, M. " Mentoring and Undergraduate Academic Success: A Literature Review," *Review of Educational Research*, 6 (1991): 505-32.

Jensen, E. L. "Student Financial Aid and Persistence in College," *Journal of Higher Education*, 52 (1981): 280-94.

Johnson, D., R. Johnson, and K. Smith. *Active Learning Cooperation in College Classrooms*. Edina, MN: Interaction Book Company, 1991.

Johnson, D., R. Johnson, and K. Smith. "Cooperative Learning Increasing College Faculty Instructional Productivity." *ASHE-ERIC Higher Education Report No 4*. Washington, DC ,The George Washington University, 1992.

Johnson, I. H., and A. J. Ottens, (Eds.) *Leveling the Playing Field: Promoting Academic Success for Students of Color*. San Francisco: Jossey-Bass, 1996.

Johnson, I. H.. "Access and Retention: Support Programs for Graduate and Professional Students," *New Directions for Student Services*, 74 (1996): 53.

Kalsner, L. "Issues in College Student Retention," *Higher Education Service Review*, 3 (1) (1991).

King, M. C. "Academic Advising, Retention, and Transfer," *New Directions for Community Colleges*, 82 (1993): 21.

Kinnick, M. K., and M. F. Ricks. "Student Retention: Moving from Numbers to Action," *Research in Higher Education*, 34(1) (1993): 55.

Kleeman, G. L. "Achieving Academic Success with Ethnically Diverse Students: Implications for Student Affairs," *NASPA Journal*, 31(2) (1994).

Kluepfel, G. A. and G. Roberts. "Introduction: Special Issue on Retention Programs," *Journal of Developmental Education*, 17(3) (1994).

Kluepfel, G. A., R. J. Parelius, and G. Roberts. "Involving Faculty in Retention," *Journal of Developmental Education*, 17(3) (1994).

Kuh, G., I. Shuh, E. Whitee, and Associates. *Involving Colleges* San Francisco: Jossey-Bass, 1991.

Kuh, G., and R. Andreas. "It's About Time: Using Qualitative Methods in Student Life Studies," *Journal of College Student Development*, 32 (1991): 397-405.

Kulik, C. I. Kulik, and B. Schwalb "College Programs for High-risk and Disadvantaged Students," *Review of Educational Research*, 53 (1983): 397-414.

Lang, M.. "Black Student Retention at Predominantly Black Institutions: Problems, Issues and Alternatives," *Western Journal of Black Studies*, 10 (2) (1986). .

Lang, M., and C. A. Ford. *Black student retention in higher education*. Springfield, IL: Charles C Thomas, 1988.

Lang, M., and C. A. Ford. (Eds.) *Strategies for Retaining Minority Students in Higher Education*. Springfield, IL: Charles C. Thomas, 1992.

Levin, M. E., and J. R. Levin. "A Critical Examination of Academic Retention Programs for At-Risk Minority College Students," *Journal of College Student Development*, 32(4) (1991): 323-34.

Lichtman, C., A. Bass, and J. Ager, Jr. "Differences Between Black and White Students in Attrition Patterns from an Urban Commuter University," *The Journal of College Student Development*, 30 (1989): 4-9.

London, H. B. "Breaking Away: A Study of First Generation College Students and Their Families," *The American Journal of Sociology*, 97 (1989): 144-70.

Loo, C. M. ,and G. Rolison. "Alienation of Ethnic Minority Students at a Predominantely White University," *Journal of Higher Education*, 57 (1986): 58-77.

Love, B. J. "Issues and Problems in the Retention of Black Students in Predominantly White Institutions of Higher Education," *Equity and Excellence in Education*, 26(1) (1993): 27.

MacGregor, J. "Collaborative Learning Shared Inquiry as a Process of Reform.". in M. Svinicki (Ed.). *The Changing Face of College Teaching. New Directions for Teaching and Learning, No. 42*. San Francisco: Jossey-Bass, 1990.

Maguire, J. "Reversing the Recent Decline in Minority Participation in Higher Education," *Minorities in Public Higher Education: At a Turning Point.* Washington, DC: American Association of State Colleges and Universities, 1988, pp. 21-41.

Manski, C., and D. Wise. *College Choice in America.* Cambridge: Harvard University Press, 1983.

Matthews, R. "Enriching Teaching and Learning Through Learning Communities," in *Teaching and Learning in the Community College.* Washington, DC: The American Association of Community Colleges, 1993.

McNairy, F. G. "The Challenge for Higher Education: Retaining Students of Color," *New Directions for Student Services*, 74 (1996): 3.

Merriam, S B., T. K. Thomas, and C. P. Zeph. "Mentoring in Higher Education: What We Know Now," *The Review of Higher Education*, 1 (1987): 199-210.

Metzner, B. "Perceived Quality of Academic Advising: The Effect on Freshman Attrition," *American Educational Research Journal*, 26 (1989): 422-442.

Miller, C. A. "Minority Student Achievement: A Comprehensive Perspective. *Journal of Developmental Education*, 13(3) (1990).

Moller-Wong, C. and A. Eide. "An Engineering Student Retention Study," *Journal of Engineering Education.* 86(1) (1997): 7.

Moore, W ., and L.C. Carpenter. A"cademically Underprepared Students," in *Increasing Student Retention*, edited by L. Noel and R. Levitz. San Francisco: Jossey-Bass, 1985.

Mortenson, T. G. "Equity of Higher Education Opportunity for Women, Black, Hispanic and Low Income Students," *An American College Testing Program Student Financial Aid Research Report*, Series 91-1, January, 1991.

Murguia, E., R. V. Padilla, and M. Pavel." Ethnicity and the Concept of Social Integration in Tinto's Model of Institutional Departure," *Journal of College Student Development*, 32 (1991): 433-9.

Naretto, J. A. "Adult Student Retention: The Influence of Internal and External Communities," *NASPA Journal*, 32(2) (1995): 90.

Nerad, M. and D. S. Miller. "Increasing Student Retention in Graduate and Professional Programs," *New Directions for Institutional Research*, 92 (1996): 61.

Nettles, M. T. Assessing Progress inMminority Access and Achievement in American Higher Education. Denver, CO: Education Commission of the States, 1991.

Nettles, M.. T., (ed.) *Toward Black Undergraduate Student Equality in American Higher Education.* Westport, Connecticut: Greenwood Press, 1988.

Noel, L., and R. Levitz (Eds.) *How to Succeed with Academically Underprepared Students.* Iowa City: American College Testing Program, 1982.

_____. *Increasing Student Retention*. San Francisco: Jossey-Bass, 1982.

Nora, A. "Determinants of Retention Among Chicano College Students," *Research in Higher Education*, 61 (1987):31-59.

_____. "Campus-Based Aid Programs as Determinants of Retention Among Hispanic Community College Students," *Journal of Higher Education*, 61 (1990): 312-31.

Nora, A., and L. Rendon. "Determinants of Predisposition to Transfer Among Community College Students," *Research in Higher Education*, 31 (1990): 235-55.

O'Neil, K. K. "An Evaluation of Student Retention Efforts at a Small College," *NASPA Journal*, 31(1) (1993): 36.

Padilla, R., and D. M. Pavel. *Successful Hispanic Community College Ctudents: An Exploratory Qualitative Study*. Tempe Hispanic Research Center, Arizona State University, 1986.

Pascarella, E. T. "Student-Faculty Informal Contact and College Outcomes," *Review of Educational Research*, 50 (1980): 545-595.

_____. "Studying Student Attrition." *New Directions for Institutional Research*. San Francisco: Jossey-Bass, 1982.

_____. "A Program for Research and Policy Development on Student Persistence at the Institutional Level." *Journal of College Student Personnel*, 27 (1986): 100-07.

Pascarella, E. T., C. Ethington, and J. Smart. 'The influence of college on humanitarian/ civic involvement values". *Journal of Higher Education*, 59 (1988): 412-437.

Pascarella, E. T., I. Smart, and J. Braxton. "Postsecondary Educational Attainment and Humanitarian and Civic Values." *Journal of College Student Personnel*, 27 (1986): 418-25.

Pascarella, E. T., and P.T. Terenzini. *How College Affects Students*. San Francisco: Jossey-Bass, 1991.

Perry, S.. "Teaching Underprepared Students Without Compromising Standards". *Chronicle of Higher Education*, 26 (1983): 25-27.

Person, D. R., and M.C. Christensen.. "Understanding Black Student Culture and Black Student Retention." *NASPA Journal*. 34(1)(1996): 47.

Peterson, R., T. Blackburn, Z. F. Gamson, C. H. Arce, R. W. Davenport, and J. R. Mingle. *Black Students on White Campuses: The Impacts of Increased Black Enrollments*. Ann Arbor, Michigan: Institute for Social Research, 1978.

Pollard, D. Black women: "Interpersonal Support and Institutional Change", in Antler and Biklen (Eds.) *Women and Change in Education*. Albany: State University of New York, 1990.

Raimst, L. *College Student Attrition and Retention*. New York: College Entrance Examination Board, 1981.

Rendon, L. I. and A. Nora. "Hispanic Student Retention in Community Colleges: Reconciling Access with Outcomes", in C. Sotello, V., Turner, M. Garcia, A. Nora, and L. Rendon (Eds.). *Racial and Ethnic Diversity in Higher Education*. Needham Heights, MA: Simon and Schuster Custom Publishing, pp. 268-80.

Richardson, C. R. *Fostering Minority Access and Achievement in Higher Education*. San Francisco: Jossey-Bass, 1987.

Richardson, R. C. *Promoting Fair College Outcomes: Learning from the Experiences of the Past Decade*. Denver, CO: Educational Commission of the States, 1991.

Richardson, R. C., D. C. Matthews, and J. E. Finney. *Improving State and Campus Environments for Quality and Diversity: A Self-Assessment*. Denver, CO: Education Commission of the States, 1992.

Richardson, R. C., and E. F. Skinner. *Achieving Quality and Diversity: Universities in a Multicultural Society*. New York: ACE/Macmillian Publishing Company, 1991.

Roueche, I. E., and G. A. Baker. *Access and Excellence*. Washington, DC: The Community College Press,1987.

Seidman, A. "Integrated Admission Counseling: Impact on Enrollment." *The Freshman Year Experience Newsletter*, 4 (1992): 6-7.

Sevier, R. A. "Those Important Things: What Every College President Needs to Know about Marketing and Student Recruiting," *College and University*, 71(4) (1996): 9.

Sheheen, F. R. "The Role of State Boards of Higher Education in Influencing Access and Retention of Minorities in Higher Education." *Peabody Journal of Education*, 66(1) (1988): 20.

Simmons, R. "Precollege Programs: A Contributing Factor to University Student Retention." *Journal of Developmental Education*, 17(3)(1988): 42.

Smith, B. L. "Taking Structure Seriously: The Learning Community Model." *Liberal Education*. 77(2)(1991): 42-8.

Smith, B. L. "Creating Learning Communities." *Liberal Education*, 79(4) (1993): 32-9.

Smith, L., et al. *Mobilizing the Campus for Retention*. The ACT National Center for the Advancement of Educational Practices, Iowa City.

Stage, F. K. " Motivation, Academic and Social Integration, and the Early Dropout." *American Educational Research Journal*, 23 (1989): 385-402.

Stampen, J. O., and A. F. Cabrera. "Exploring the Effects of Student Aid on Attrition." *The Journal of Student Financial Aid*, 16 (1986): 28-40.

Stewart, G., R. B. Russell, and D. B. Wright. "The Comprehensive Role of Student Affairs in African-American Student Retention." *The Journal of College Admissions*, 154 (1987): 6.

Stodt, M. M. and W. M. Klepper. *Increasing Retention: Academic and Student Affairs Administrators in Partnership*. San Francisco: Jossey-Bass, 1987.

Suen, H. K. "Alienation and Attrition of Black College Students on a Predominantly White Campus." *Journal of College Student Personnel*, 24 (1983): 117-21.

Swift, Jr.,I. S. "Retention of Adult College Students." *National Academic Advising Association Journal*, 7 (1987): 7-19.

Tate, D. S., and C. L. Schwartz. "Increasing the Retention of American Indian Students in Professional Programs in Higher Education." *Journal of American Indian Education*. 33(1) (1993): 21.

Terenzini, P. T., W. Lorang, and E. T. Pascarella. "Predicting Freshman Persistence and Voluntary Dropout Decisions: A Replication." *Research in Higher Education*, 15 (1981): 109-127.

Thompson, C. E., and B. R. Fretz. "Predicting the Adjustment of Black Students at Predominantly White Institutions." *Journal of Higher Education* 62 (1991): 437-50.

Tinto, V. *Leaving College: Rethinking the Causes and Cures of Student Attrition* (Second Edition). Chicago: University of Chicago Press, 1993.

Tinto, V., A. Goodsell-Love, and P. Russo. *Building Community Among New College Students*. University Park, Pennsylvania: The National Center on Postsecondary Teaching, Learning and Assessment, The Pennsylvania State University, 1994.

Tinto, V., and P. Russo. "Coordinated Studies Programs: The Effect on Student Involvement at a Community College." *Community College Review*, 1993.

Turnbull, W. W. "Involvement: The Key to Retention." *Journal of Developmental Education*, 10(2) (1986).

Upcraft, M. L., J. Gardner, and Associates. *The Freshman Year Experience*. San Francisco: Jossey-Bass Publishers, 1989.

Valverde, L. " Low Income Students." *Increasing Student Retention*, edited by L. Noel and R. Levitz. San Francisco: Jossey-Bass, 1985.

Williams, T. M., and M. M. Leonard. "Graduating Black Undergraduates: the Step Beyond Retention." *Journal of College Student Development*, 29 (1988): 69-75.

Williamson, D., and D. Creamer. "Student Attrition in Two and Four-Year Colleges: Application of a Theoretical Model." *Journal of College Student Development*, 28 (1988): 197-217.

Winston, R. B., S. C. Ender, and T. K. Miller. "Academic Advising as Student Development," in *New Directions for Student Services Developmental Approaches to Academic Advising*. San Francisco: Jossey-Bass, 1982.

Yess, l. P. "Community College Students Never Drop Out." *Community College Review*, 7 (1970): 56-9.

Youn, D. K.. Student Retention: Many More Ideas." *College Student Journal*, 26(4) (1992): 472.